OFFICE

OUTLAWS, MOBSTERS &CROOKS

ISSN 1540-739X

OUTLAWS, MOBSTERS &CROOKS

From the Old West to the Internet

VOLUME 5

Marie J. MacNee
Edited by Sarah Hermsen and Allison McNeill

Detroit • New York • San Diego • San Francisco • Cleveland • New Haven, Conn. • Waterville, Maine • London • Munich

THOMSON
™
GALE

Outlaws, Mobsters & Crooks: From the Old West to the Internet, Volume 5

Marie J. MacNee

Project Editors
Sarah Hermsen, Allison McNeill

Permissions
Lori Hines

Imaging and Multimedia
Kelly A. Quin, Robert Duncan

Product Design
Michelle DiMercurio, Tracey Rowens, Cynthia Baldwin

Composition
Evi Seoud

Manufacturing
Rita Wimberley

ISBN 0-7876-6483-9
ISSN 1540-739X

Printed in the United States of America
10 9 8 7 6 5 4 3 2 1

Contents

Reader's Guide

"History is nothing more than a tableau of crimes and misfortunes," wrote eighteenth-century French writer Voltaire. There certainly is more to history than criminal deeds, misdemeanors, and misfortunes, but these offenses do offer fascinating lessons in history. The life stories of outlaws provide a glimpse into other times and other places, as well as provocative insight into contemporary issues.

WHO'S INCLUDED

Outlaws, Mobsters & Crooks, Volume 5, presents the life stories of twenty-three outlaws who lived (or committed crimes) from the nineteenth century to the present day—from The Dalton Gang, who robbed banks in the late 1800s, to terrorist Timothy McVeigh.

Everyone's familiar with John Gotti, the Sundance Kid, and Lizzie Borden. But how many know the *whole* story: what their childhoods were like, what their first crime was, who worked with them—and against them—and how they ended up? *Outlaws, Mobsters & Crooks* offers a thorough and provocative look at the people and events involved in these stories.

Familiar figures such as Pretty Boy Floyd and Byron de la Beckwith are present, as are lesser-known outlaws whose careers reveal much about the times in which they lived. David Smith, for instance, created a computer virus called Melissa that disrupted operations for as many as one million users, showing how susceptible computers in the twentieth century could be to viruses. Also included are criminals such as Charles Whitman, whose crime was an event—the University of Texas tower shooting—that is remembered more than his name, and lawmen who sometimes stood on the wrong side of the law. The many men and women who have been labeled outlaws over the course of three centuries cannot all be profiled in one volume. But those whose stories are told in *Outlaws, Mobsters & Crooks,* Volume 5, includes some of the best-known, least-known, weirdest, scariest, most despised, and least understood outlaws. In short, this work is intended as an overview of criminals—a jumping-off point for further inquiry.

Also included are updates of four criminals from the first four volumes of *Outlaws, Mobsters & Crooks,* where you'll find recent information about mobster John Gotti, terrorist Timothy McVeigh, and others. You'll learn who's been pardoned, whose parole was denied, and what some of these onetime crooks are up to now.

LEGENDS, MYTHS, AND OUTRIGHT LIES

Many of the men and women profiled in Volume 5 have been surrounded by legends that have grown to enormous proportions, making it difficult to separate fact from fiction. For example, Lizzie Borden, who was never convicted of her father's murder, was rumored to have given him "forty-one whacks" with an axe when in reality he was struck ten times. In some cases, legends have grown out of fictionalized contemporary accounts. Others stem from stories distorted by the criminals themselves, the lawmen who pursued them, and even the families and friends of both victims and perpetrators. Some are accurate first-person accounts. Others are sensational exaggerations of true events. And some are wholesale fabrications.

Outlaws, Mobsters & Crooks, Volume 5, attempts to present a fair and complete account of what is known about the lives and activities of twenty-three outlaws. When appropriate, entries mention the myths, unconventional theories, and alternate versions of accepted history that apply to a particular criminal—without suggesting that they are either truthful or based in fact.

ARRANGEMENT AND PRESENTATION

Outlaws, Mobsters & Crooks, Volume 5, is a continuation of U•X•L's 4-volume *Outlaws, Mobsters & Crooks* series. The biographies are arranged alphabetically by the criminal's last name or by the first letter in their better known nickname, as in the cases of Pretty Boy Floyd and the Sundance Kid. The entries range from three to eleven pages in length, and include given names and aliases, birth and death information, and portraits of the subjects as well as additional photos.

Entries are lively, easy to read, and written in a straightforward style that is geared to challenge—but not frustrate—students. Difficult words are defined within the text; some words also have pronunciations listed. Technical words and legal terms are also explained within entries, enabling students to learn the vocabulary appropriate to a particular subject without having to consult other sources for definitions.

WHAT'S INSIDE

What's inside is a detailed look at what they did, why they did it, and how their stories ended. Entries focus on the entire picture—not just the headline news—to provide the following sorts of information:

- **Personal background:** interesting details about the subject's family, upbringing, and youth

- **Crimes and misdeeds:** an in-depth look at the subject's criminal history

- **Aftermath:** from jail time, to legal and illegal executions, to mysterious disappearances, entries relate what happened after the dirty deeds were done

- **A look at the other side of the law:** extensive information on the other side of the law—the lawmen and others who were involved in the pursuit, capture, or prosecution of the outlaw profiled

ADDED FEATURES

Outlaws, Mobsters & Crooks, Volume 5, includes a number of additional features that help make the connection between people, places, and historic events.

- Update entries keep readers current on selected criminals profiled in *Outlaws, Mobsters & Crooks,* Volumes 1 to 4.

- A timeline at the beginning of the volume provides a listing of outlaw landmarks and important international events.

- Sidebars provide fascinating supplemental information, such as sketches of criminal associates, profiles of law enforcement officials and agencies, and explanations of the political and social scenes of the era. Sidebars also offer a contemporary perspective of people and events through excerpts of letters written by the criminal profiled, citations from newspapers and journals of the day, and much more.

- Quotes—both by and about the outlaws—provide insight into what motivated them.

- 46 photographs and illustrations bring the outlaws to life.

- Suggestions for related books and movies—both fictional and fact-based—are liberally sprinkled throughout the entries.

- A list of sources for more information at the end of each entry includes books, newspaper and magazine articles, and Internet addresses for additional and bibliographical information.

- A comprehensive index at the end of the volume provides easy access to the people, places, and events mentioned throughout all five volumes of *Outlaws, Mobsters & Crooks*.

SPECIAL THANKS

The author would like to thank U•X•L Project Editors Sarah Hermsen and Allison McNeill and Permissions Specialist Lori Hines and Image Editor Kelly A. Quin of Gale for their invaluable help and guidance. The author would also like to extend a special thanks to Sarah Gwisdalla, for her boundless enthusiasm and conscientious research. This book is dedicated, again, with love and appreciation, to the author's parents.

COMMENTS AND SUGGESTIONS

We welcome your comments on *Outlaws, Mobsters & Crooks: From the Old West to the Internet,* Volume 5, and suggestions for other criminals to be featured in future editions. Please write: Editors, *Outlaws, Mobsters & Crooks,* U•X•L, 27500 Drake Road, Farmington Hills, Michigan, 48331-3535; call toll-free: 800-877-4253; fax to: 248-699-8097; or send e-mail via http://www.gale.com.

Outlaws by Category

Italic numbers indicate volume numbers.
Boldface type indicates main entries in *Outlaws, Mobsters & Crooks*,
Volume 5. Volumes 1, 2, 3, and 4 refer to the prior four volumes in the set.
 indicates an update to an original entry.

BANDITS AND GUNSLINGERS

BOOTLEGGERS

COMPUTER CRIMINALS

MOBSTERS

Robbers

Spies

Swindlers

Terrorists

Trespassers

Timeline

May 11, 1853: California's Governor John Bigler approves an act to appoint a company of mounted rangers to capture a gang of Mexican robbers. He offers $1,000 reward for the capture—dead or alive—of any Mexican named Joaquin.

1889: Butch Cassidy, **the Sundance Kid,** and the rest of the Wild Bunch launch a series of robberies that will continue until 1901.

August 4, 1892: Andrew and Sarah Borden are found dead in their home, bludgeoned to death with an axe.

October 5, 1892: Bob, Grattan, and Emmett Dalton—**the Dalton Gang**—attempt to rob two banks in their former hometown of Coffeyville, Kansas.

June 5, 1893: Lizzie Borden is put on trial for the bloody murder of her parents. On June 20, the jury announces a verdict of not guilty.

October 21, 1897: Harry Longabaugh, a.k.a. **the Sundance Kid,** escapes from jail while awaiting trial for robbing a bank in South Dakota.

February 14, 1905: Two English-speaking bandits hold up a bank in Argentina. Pinkerton detectives believe the two robbers are Butch Cassidy and **the Sundance Kid.**

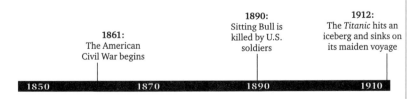

1861:
The American
Civil War begins

1890:
Sitting Bull is
killed by U.S.
soldiers

1912:
The *Titanic* hits an
iceberg and sinks on
its maiden voyage

| 1850 | 1870 | 1890 | 1910 |

November 7, 1908: Two foreigners are killed in a shoot-out with a posse of Bolivian soldiers; many believe the robbers to have been Butch Cassidy and the **Sundance Kid.**

November 1923: Nathan Leopold and Richard Loeb begin to plot "the perfect crime."

May 21, 1924: **Leopold and Loeb** kidnap and kill fourteen-year-old Bobby Franks.

July 21, 1924: The trial of **Leopold and Loeb** begins.

September 10, 1924: Leopold and Loeb are convicted of the murder of Bobby Franks; both are sentenced to life in prison.

1925: Pretty Boy Floyd robs a payroll in St. Louis, Missouri, for which he is sentenced to three years in a state penitentiary.

1926: William Sutton Jr. and Eddie Wilson abort their attempt to rob a bank in Queens, New York. Arrested, Sutton is sentenced to five to ten years in prison.

August 1929: Bank robber **William Sutton Jr.** is granted parole following a prison riot at Dannemora prison in northeast New York.

1930: Pretty Boy Floyd is convicted of robbing a bank in Sylvania, Ohio, for which he is sentenced to ten to twenty-five years in the state penitentiary.

June 1, 1932: Robber **William Sutton Jr.** is returned to jail; he escapes six months later.

1933: William Sutton Jr. is sentenced to do time in Pennsylvania's Eastern State Prison.

June 17, 1933: A squad of police officers is ambushed in Kansas City, Missouri. Accused of participating in the massacre, **Pretty Boy Floyd** denies any involvement.

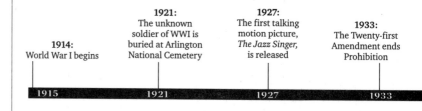

1914:
World War I begins

1921:
The unknown soldier of WWI is buried at Arlington National Cemetery

1927:
The first talking motion picture, *The Jazz Singer,* is released

1933:
The Twenty-first Amendment ends Prohibition

1915   1921   1927   1933

Outlaws, Mobsters & Crooks

November 27, 1934: Outlaw **Pretty Boy Floyd** is killed in a shoot-out with FBI agents.

January 28, 1936: Convicted child killer **Richard Loeb** is killed by a fellow inmate.

1938: Mobster **Raymond Patriarca** is arrested for participating in the robbery of a Massachusetts jewelry store, for which he is sentenced to three to five years in a state prison.

1941: Massachusetts Governor's Councilor Daniel H. Coakley is removed from office for his role in corrupt political practices after an investigation into the early release of **Raymond Patriarca.**

February 3, 1947: William Sutton Jr. and four others escape from Holmesburg, a maximum-security prison once considered to be escape-proof.

March 9, 1950: William Sutton Jr. robs the Manufacturer's Trust Bank in New York of $60,000.

February 10, 1952: Twenty-four-year-old Arnold Schuster spots robber **William Sutton Jr.** on a train to Brooklyn, New York. He alerts authorities and is later found shot to death. Sutton is later convicted of robbery, for which he is sentenced to a minimum of thirty years in prison.

1954: Philip Bucola, head of the New England Crime Family, flees to Sicily, allowing **Raymond Patriarca** to assume leadership.

May 13, 1958: Granted parole, **Nathan Leopold** is released from prison.

August 1, 1961: Charles Whitman shoots randomly from a tower on the University of Texas campus, killing fifteen and wounding thirty-one others before being killed by police.

1963: Fifteen-year-old **Frank Abagnale Jr.** pulls his first scam—with his father as the victim.

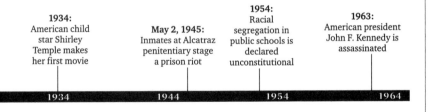

1934: American child star Shirley Temple makes her first movie

May 2, 1945: Inmates at Alcatraz penitentiary stage a prison riot

1954: Racial segregation in public schools is declared unconstitutional

1963: American president John F. Kennedy is assassinated

1934   1944   1954   1964

June 12, 1963: Byron de la Beckwith assassinates Medgar Evers, a field secretary in the National Association for the Advancement of Colored People (NAACP).

June 20, 1967: Mobster **Raymond Patriarca** and two others are indicted in federal court for conspiring to murder a Rhode Island bookie.

March 1969: Mobster **Raymond Patriarca** enters prison.

December 24, 1969: Bank robber **Willie Sutton** is released from prison.

January 9, 1975: After serving six years of his sentence, mobster **Raymond Patriarca** is granted early parole.

1978: Mobster **Raymond Patriarca** is accused of being involved in a plot to assassinate Cuban leader Fidel Castro.

1980: Con artist **Frank Abagnale Jr.** publishes his autobiography *Catch Me If You Can*.

November 2, 1980: Bank robber **William Sutton Jr.** dies and is buried in an unmarked grave in the family plot in Brooklyn.

1981: Mobster **Raymond Patriarca** is indicted by a grand jury in Miami, Florida, on charges of labor racketeering.

1982: A civilian employee of the Naval Intelligence Service, **Jonathan Jay Pollard** begins to use his access to classified information to help Israel.

July 11, 1984: New England crime boss **Raymond Patriarca** dies of a heart attack at the age of seventy-six.

November 21, 1985: Fearful of being arrested for espionage, **Jonathan Jay Pollard** requests political asylum at the Israeli embassy in Washington, D.C. He and his wife are denied entry.

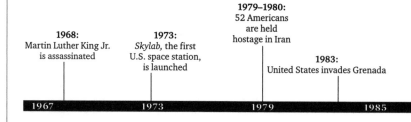

1968:
Martin Luther King Jr. is assassinated

1973:
Skylab, the first U.S. space station, is launched

1979–1980:
52 Americans are held hostage in Iran

1983:
United States invades Grenada

1967   1973   1979   1985

March 1986: A routine federal audit reveals that Lincoln Savings and Loan, run by **Charles Keating Jr.**, had broken an "equity rule" that limited how much a savings and loan institution could directly invest.

1987: Convicted of treason, **Jonathan Jay Pollard** receives the maximum sentence: life in a federal penitentiary.

June 2, 1987: Katya Komisaruk breaks into Vandenberg Air Force Base in California and destroys a government computer, leaving behind cookies, flowers, and a poem. She is later arrested by police and charged with sabotage and destruction of government property.

July 5, 1987: Wealthy Manhattan socialite Irene Silverman disappears; **Sante and Kenneth Kimes** are soon linked to her disappearance.

1989: After serving only three years of a five-year sentence, **Sante Kimes** is released from prison.

April 12, 1989: American Continental, the parent company of Lincoln Savings and Loan, files for bankruptcy protection.

May 7, 1989: Greg and **Pamela Smart** are married in Lowell, Massachusetts.

May 1, 1990: Greg Smart, married to **Pamela Smart** less than a year, is murdered by his wife's teenage lover and his accomplices.

June 10, 1990: Vance Lattime Sr., the father of one of the boys who participated in the murder of Greg Smart, surrenders his gun collection to police after suspecting his son's involvement.

July 13, 1990: Pamela Smart's friend, Cecilia Pierce, wears a wire to record incriminating conversations.

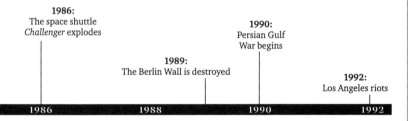

1986:
The space shuttle
Challenger explodes

1989:
The Berlin Wall is destroyed

1990:
Persian Gulf
War begins

1992:
Los Angeles riots

1986   1988   1990   1992

1991: The state of California convicts **Charles Keating Jr.** of seventeen counts of securities fraud, for which he is sentenced to ten years in prison.

1993: Activist **Katya Komisaruk** earns a law degree from Harvard Law School and is admitted to the California Bar.

1994: Lawyers representing **Jonathan Jay Pollard,** who is serving a life term for treason, request leniency from President Bill Clinton. The request is denied.

1994: Tried for a third time, **Byron de la Beckwith** is convicted of the murder of Medgar Evers, for which the seventy-three-year-old is sentenced to life in prison.

1995: Dubbed "the year of the spy" because of the number of intelligence leaks from United States government agents.

1995: Boston mobster/informant **James Bulger** disappears, leaving the FBI perplexed.

1995: Imprisoned Mafia don **John Gotti** is diagnosed with terminal cancer.

January 1995: A Boston grand jury indicts **James Bulger** and five others on charges of extortion and racketeering.

July 27, 1996: A bomb explodes in Centennial Park during the Olympic Games in Atlanta, Georgia.

1997: A prison parole board meets to decide whether convicted spy **Christopher Boyce** should be granted parole. The board recommends that Boyce be released to a halfway house in September 2002.

January 16, 1997: A bomb explodes at an abortion clinic in Atlanta, Georgia, injuring six people. Agents eventually identify **Eric Robert Rudolph**—previously linked to the 1996 Olympic Games bombing—as the primary suspect.

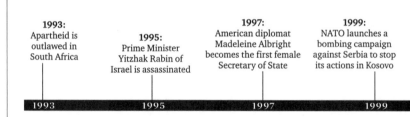

1993:
Apartheid is outlawed in South Africa

1995:
Prime Minister Yitzhak Rabin of Israel is assassinated

1997:
American diplomat Madeleine Albright becomes the first female Secretary of State

1999:
NATO launches a bombing campaign against Serbia to stop its actions in Kosovo

| 1993 | 1995 | 1997 | 1999 |

1999: Former convict/attorney-activist **Katya Komisaruk** advises protesters at the World Trade Organization (WTO) conference in Seattle, Washington.

March 26, 1999: Transmitted in only three minutes, the Melissa computer virus spreads across the globe to computers in Belgium, Germany, China, and elsewhere. More than one million computers—including hundreds of networks—are affected by the virus.

April 1999: Charles Keating Jr. makes a deal with prosecutors, pleading guilty to four counts of fraud.

April 1, 1999: Identified as the author of the Melissa virus, computer hacker **David Smith** is arrested in New Jersey.

December 10, 1999: David Smith is found guilty of computer theft and damaging computer programs or data.

May 18, 2000: Mother and son team **Sante and Kenneth Kimes** are convicted of 118 criminal counts, ranging from conspiracy to robbery, eavesdropping, illegal weapons possession, and murder; each is sentenced to more than one hundred years in prison.

September 2000: James Bulger, still a fugitive, is indicted by a federal grand jury for his involvement in eighteen murders.

June 11, 2001: Oklahoma City bomber **Timothy McVeigh** is executed by lethal injection in Terre Haute, Indiana.

June 10, 2002: John Gotti dies from throat cancer at a federal prison hospital in Springfield, Missouri.

2000:
George W. Bush wins the U.S. presidency in a hotly contested election

September 11, 2001:
Terrorists attack the World Trade Center and the Pentagon

2002:
U.S. Justice Department launches a probe into the bankruptcy scandel involving energy giant Enron

2000   2001   2002

OUTLAWS, MOBSTERS &CROOKS

Frank Abagnale Jr.

April 27, 1948
AKA: Frank Williams
Swindler

At age sixteen, Frank Abagnale left home in search of recognition and excitement. After forging identity documents, he impersonated an airline pilot. For two years, and in cities all over the United States and Europe, he used the power of his pilot uniform to pass phony checks at airports and hotels. Abagnale's autobiography, *Catch Me If You Can,* describes how he assumed several other scam occupations, playing the parts of professor, pediatrician, stockbroker, and lawyer. He was dubbed "the world's greatest con man" by the *Wall Street Journal.* Through his various fake jobs, Abagnale collected $2.5 million in five years, before he was captured in France. He served time there and in Sweden before entering the U.S. correctional system. After serving five years of his American prison sentence, he was released on the condition that he advise authorities such as the Federal Bureau of Investigation (FBI) on ways to stay ahead of thieves like him. He now runs his own consulting firm and is the subject of the 2002 film, *Catch Me If You Can,* based on his 1980 memoir.

"Frank Abagnale could write a check on toilet paper...sign it 'U.R. Hooked' and cash it at any bank in town."

--Former Houston police chief, quoted in *Catch Me If You Can*

LIFE WITH FATHER

The third of four children, Frank Abagnale was raised in Bronxville, New York. His father, Frank, and mother, Paulette, a French-Algerian woman, met and married during World War II (1939–45), while Frank Sr. was serving in the U.S. armed forces. He was twenty-eight; she was fifteen.

After returning from the war, Frank Sr. opened a successful stationery business called Gramercy. The family lived in a luxurious large home in an upscale neighborhood and they enjoyed a comfortable lifestyle. Actively involved in politics and an avid deep-sea fisherman, Frank Sr. was frequently away from home. During one of his out-of-state fishing trips, his wife left and took the children with her. After Paulette divorced Frank Sr., their twelve-year-old son, Frank Jr., went to live with his father.

Life with father provided an interesting education. Frank Jr. met politicians, went to bars, and learned what he could from the experience of others. He became friends with delinquents and landed in trouble with the law. But thanks to his father's political connections, Frank Jr.'s juvenile record remained unblemished.

By age fifteen, Frank Abagnale Jr. had what he called "girl crazies"—a state of mind that soon led to his first moneymaking scam. He asked his father for a credit card to pay for gas and his father obliged. The young con artist took his father's Mobil card to gas stations throughout the Bronx, where he persuaded station attendants to run charges for repairs they never made. Instead, they handed over the charged amount to Abagnale, who shared a portion of the money with his accomplices.

Abagnale's 1980 autobiography describes the thrill of his first success:

> I was heady with happiness. Since I hadn't yet had my first taste of alcohol, I couldn't compare the feeling to a champagne high, but it was the most delightful sensation I'd ever experienced in the front seat of a car.

> In fact, my cleverness overwhelmed me. If it worked once, why wouldn't it work twice? It did. It worked so many times in the next several weeks, I lost count.

In the end, Abagnale scammed his father out of $34,000 in phony charges. Neither his father nor mother were pleased with

Self Knowledge

"Modesty is not one of my virtues. Virtue is not one of my virtues."
--Frank Abagnale, quoted in *Entertainment Weekly*

his ingenuity. Paulette arranged to have her son sent to a Catholic Charities reformatory, hoping that strict discipline would straighten him out.

But Abagnale hated the reformatory, and left after only one year to return to live with his father. But his father's life was now very different. Frank Sr., who once wore expensive suits and drove luxury cars, was financially ruined. He lived on the modest salary of a postal clerk and drove a beat-up old car. It was not a lifestyle the younger Abagnale embraced.

Sleazy Is as Sleazy Does

When the *Denver Business Journal* asked Abagnale to describe his favorite con, he cited a scam perpetrated by two New Jersey teenagers. The teens placed an ad in the newspaper promising X-rated videos at bargain prices. In taking orders, they accepted only checks and money orders, which require a signature and can be traced to the person who wrote them. After receiving orders, the teens wrote back to customers to inform them that the videos were no longer in stock. They included a refund on a company check. "The catch was the company name," Abagnale said. "Child Pornography Videos Inc. was printed in large red letters in the upper left corner. This proved to be too embarrassing for the customers and none of the refund checks were ever cashed."

THE MAKING OF A PAPERHANGER

At age sixteen, Abagnale left home. He said goodbye to no one and left no notes behind. He later explained his reasons for leaving in his autobiography: "One June morning of 1964, I woke up and knew it was time to go. Some remote corner of the world seemed to be whispering, 'Come.' So I went."

That remote corner of the world turned out to be New York City, where Abagnale conned another boy's parents into letting him stay with them. As a sixteen-year-old high school dropout, his employment opportunities were limited. He landed a minimum-wage job, but found he could barely support himself. Abagnale decided that his age was preventing him from finding better work, so he doctored his identification papers to show that he was a man in his mid-twenties. And at well over six feet tall, he easily passed for the older age.

But Abagnale's lack of education continued to hold him back. Earning only $2.50 an hour, he began to write bad checks to supplement his income. "After two months of cranking out worthless checks, however, I faced myself with some unpleasant truths," Abagnale later wrote. "I was a crook. Nothing more,

The Power of a Uniform

"There is enchantment in a uniform, especially one that marks the wearer as a person of rare skills, courage or achievement. A paratrooper's wings tell of a special breed of soldier. A submariner's dolphin denotes the unusual sailor. A policeman's blue symbolizes authority. A forest ranger's raiment [clothing] evokes wilderness lore. Even a doorman's gaudy garb stirs vague thoughts of pomp and royalty." —Frank Abagnale, in *Catch Me If You Can*

nothing less. In the parlance [speech] of the streets, I had become a professional paperhanger. That didn't bother me too much, for I was a successful paperhanger, and at the moment to be a success at anything was the most important factor in the world to me."

A FOX ON A TURKEY RANCH

Abagnale became increasingly bold in his scams. He created false identities and posed as various professionals. His first fake occupation was that of a pilot for Pan Am airlines. He managed to get a pilot's uniform, without paying for it, by conning an airline official and a store clerk. Next, he forged an airline ID card and went to Pan Am's commissary. Dressed as a pilot, he claimed that he was not wearing his wings (a pin signifying his rank with the airline) because his child had taken them. Abagnale left the airline facility with pilot's wings. But to play his role convincingly, he needed information. To learn what he thought he needed to know about a pilot's life, he quizzed pilots about their profession.

In his autobiography Abagnale described the power of a uniform and notes its effect on others—and himself:

> I felt great in my Pan Am pilot's uniform as I walked into [New York City's] LaGuardia airport. I obviously was commanding respect and esteem. Men looked at me admiringly and enviously. Pretty women and girls smiled at me. Airport policemen nodded courteously. Pilots and stewardesses smiled at me, spoke to me, or lifted a hand in greeting as they passed. Every man, woman and child who noticed me seemed warm and friendly.

> It was heady stuff and I loved it. In fact, I became instantly addicted. During the next five years the uniform was my alter-ego. I used it in the same manner a junkie shoots up on heroin.

Posing as a pilot, Abagnale circulated through the airport, stopping at various airline counters to cash phony checks. "I

worked LaGuardia like a fox on a turkey ranch," he later told *Fortune* magazine. "I'd cash a check at the Eastern Air Line counter, for instance, then go to another section of the terminal and tap some other airline's till [cash register].... I was producing rubber [bounced checks] faster than a Ceylon planter [a rubber tree planter on the island of Sri Lanka]." For two years he posed as a pilot, while never actually piloting a plane, riding free on Pan Am flights and staying in hotels where the airline picked up the bill. Meanwhile, he passed bad checks wherever he went.

Disguised as a Pan Am pilot, Frank Abagnale rode free on Pan Am flights and had the airline pay his hotel bills.
Reproduced by permission of AP/Wide World Photos.

Paging Doctor Fox

After successfully posing as an airline pilot, Abagnale decided to keep a low profile for a while. He moved to Riverbend, a well-to-do suburb of Atlanta, Georgia. As he filled out an application to rent an apartment, he paused to consider whether he should claim pilot as his occupation. He decided against it. Instead, he wrote that he was a medical doctor.

Posing as a California doctor on leave to do research at Atlanta's Emory University, Abagnale, who became known as "Doc," carefully avoided his neighbors' requests for medical advice. But when a new tenant stopped by his apartment to introduce himself, Abagnale was forced to play the part in earnest. Coincidentally, his new neighbor was chief pediatric resident at Smithers Pediatric Institute and General Hospital. Concerned that he might be revealed as a fake, Abagnale spent time at the library, reading medical journals, books, and other materials to become knowledgeable about his supposed area of expertise—pediatrics (children's medicine).

Young "Doctor" Abagnale's dedication did not go unnoticed. When one of the staff doctors left for a family emergency, a Smithers Hospital administrator asked Abagnale to act as temporary resident supervisor. Convinced that the position would expose his lack of medical skills, he declined. But when the administrator informed him that he would not be required to practice and would only do administrative work, Abagnale accepted the assignment. He was paid handsomely.

After leaving the hospital, he decided it was time to leave the city. "There was no compulsion for me to go; at least I felt none, but I felt it [was] unwise to stay," he later wrote in his autobiography. "The fox who keeps to the same den is the easiest caught by the terriers, and I felt I had nested too long in one place. I knew I was still being hunted and I didn't want to make it easy for the hounds."

JUDAS WORE A SKIRT

After moving to another southern city, Abagnale returned to the role of a pilot. But this time, he also claimed he was a Harvard Law School graduate who had decided to pursue a more exciting profession. Once again, he convincingly played the role. While at a party, he met an assistant to the U.S. attorney general (the nation's chief law officer), who informed Abagnale that their office was looking to hire more attorneys.

To take on his new role as lawyer, Abagnale had to pass the state's bar exam—a written test that determines if a person is qualified to practice law. It is not unusual for aspiring lawyers to take the bar exam more than once before passing it. Abagnale, whose reported 136 IQ (intelligence quotient) is well above average, passed the test on his third try. He was hired by the attorney general's office and was eventually allowed to try cases, many of which he won.

After pulling off another successful scam, Abagnale decided it was time to move on. He headed for France, where he settled in the southern city of Montpellier. But his past caught up with him after he was spotted by an Air France flight attendant he had dated. The former girlfriend notified the police, who used Abagnale's license plate number to track down his whereabouts.

SHOPPING FOR TROUBLE

As Abagnale checked out of a supermarket where he often shopped, he left the counter to pick up another item. When he returned, he found neither customers nor store clerks. Instead, the counter was surrounded by French police, who knew that the man posing as an ordinary citizen was in fact the master impostor Frank Abagnale.

Abagnale was just twenty-one at the time of his arrest. During the course of his five-year "career" as a scam artist, he had defrauded victims in fifty states and twenty-six countries of a total of $2.5 million. He was first tried in France, where he served six months in prison. Next, he was extradited (turned over as a prisoner) to Sweden, where he was also tried and convicted. But his Swedish sentence was anything but hard time for Abagnale. He was sent, for about eighteen months, to a prison facility that was like a country inn and his time there was vaca-

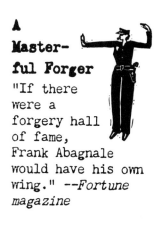

Child's Play?

"What I did 35 years ago is now 800 times easier to do today. Back when I did the things I did, it took a great deal of planning. You had to learn how to print, do color separations, make negatives, plates, etc. Today, due to technology, color copiers, scanners, computers, ink jet printers, make it child's play." —Frank Abagnale, quoted at spielbergfilms.com

A Master- ful Forger

"If there were a forgery hall of fame, Frank Abagnale would have his own wing." --*Fortune magazine*

Once a Con Artist, Always a Con Artist

After being released from prison, Abagnale continued to stage cons—tricking unwitting victims in front of television cameras. In one case, Abagnale asked a television station to choose any bank. Wearing an expensive suit, he arrived at the bank in a chauffeured limousine. He gave a teller a check written on a paper napkin. With hidden cameras rolling, the teller cashed the check. According to the journal *Drug Topics,* after learning of the con, the teller responded: "I would have cashed a check [for him] written on toilet paper."

In another instance, Abagnale scammed ABC-TV newscaster Sam Donaldson. During an interview with Donaldson, the former conman showed the newscaster a letter of recommendation. Donaldson found the letter intriguing: it appeared to have been written by Donaldson himself—on his personal stationery. But he had never written any such letter; Abagnale had created another convincing forgery.

tion-like. A sympathetic Swedish authority did Abagnale a tremendous favor when he revoked the conman's passport; without identification papers, he was deported to the United States. He had narrowly escaped extradition to Italy, where he was also wanted and where prison conditions are harsh.

But as he was returning to the United States by airplane, Abagnale managed to pry up a bathroom toilet and drop onto the runway just as the plane landed. His escape was short lived. He was caught, turned over for trial, and sentenced. Once again, he got off easy. After serving only three years of his sentence in the United States, he was released—on the condition that he assist authorities in thwarting forgers and other con artists.

FROM GROCERY CLERK TO CELEBRITY

Once free, Abagnale found his employment options were limited. He worked at a grocery store and as a movie projectionist before finding his true calling as a security consultant. Through his successful firm Abagnale & Associates, he receives requests to deliver about three hundred presentations each year. Of these, he accepts about half. In his new role, he boasts of consulting with 65 percent of the Fortune 500 companies (the largest and most profitable companies in America) and fifty of the largest banks in the United States. He also holds a teaching position at the FBI Academy.

A frequent guest on the talk show circuit, Abagnale has appeared on the Oprah Winfrey show and other popular programs. Shortly after the publication of his second autobiography, *The Art of the Steal,* director Steven Spielberg's production company began working on a movie about Abagnale's life. The film, written by *Rush Hour* screenwriter Jeff Nathanson and starring Leonardo DiCaprio and Tom Hanks, is based on Abagnale's first autobiography, *Catch Me If You Can.*

Abagnale claims to be unimpressed with his celebrity. "I have been married for over 25 years and I am the proud father of three sons," he wrote on his Web site. "When I was twenty-eight years old, I thought it would be great to have a movie about my life, but when I was twenty-eight, like when I was sixteen, I was egotistical and self-centered. We all grow up. Hopefully we get wiser. Age brings wisdom and fatherhood changes one's life completely."

For More Information

Abagnale, Frank W. *The Art of the Steal: How to Protect Yourself and Your Business from Fraud, America's #1 Crime.* New York: Broadway Books, 2001, 2002.

Abagnale & Associates. http://www.abagnale.com (accessed on March 31, 2002).

Abagnale, Frank W., with Stan Redding. *Catch Me If You Can: The Amazing True Story of the Youngest and Most Daring Con Man in the History of Fun and Profit.* New York: Broadway Books, 1980, 2000.

"Catch Me If You Can." *DreamWorks SKG Fansite.* http://www.spielberg-dreamworks.com/catchmeifyoucan/ (accessed on July 26, 2002).

Charles, Harry. Review of *The Art of the Steal: How to Protect Yourself and Your Business from Fraud—America's #1 Crime,* by Frank Abagnale. *Library Journal* (October 1, 2001).

Conlan, Michael F. "Con Man Reveals White-Collar Crime Secrets to R.Ph.s." *Drug Topics* (December 16, 1991).

Diamond, Michael. "Expert Tips Treasurers Off to Check-Fraud Scams." *Cincinnati Business Courier* (October 4, 1993).

Hicks, L. Wayne. "Ex-Con Man Now Teaches." *Denver Business Journal* (August 17, 2001).

Leonard, Devin. "Con's Checkered Past Gets Hollywood Treatment." *Fortune* (July 10, 2000).

Munro, Don. "Con Man's Career Is Grist for Crime-Fighting Course." *American Banker* (August 5, 1986).

Nashawaty, Chris. "Double Identity: A Seasoned Con Tells How He Made Millions Pretending to Be a Pilot and a Doctor in *Catch Me If You Can*." *Entertainment Weekly* (August 11, 2000).

Lizzie Borden

July 19, 1860
June 1, 1927

Accused Murderer

Lizzie Borden's father and stepmother were murdered violently in the small New England house the family shared. Lizzie, an unmarried thirty-two-year old, was arrested and tried for the murders. Because the evidence against her was circumstantial and because her calm demeanor in the courtroom contradicted the image of her as a cold-blooded killer (she even fainted when pictures of the bodies were shown in court), she was eventually cleared of the charges. However, public opinion about the trial divided the nation.

A WEALTHY PENNY-PINCHER

Andrew Jackson Borden and his wife, Sarah Anthony Borden, had three children—Emma, Lizzie, and Alice. Alice died in infancy and when Lizzie was two and Emma was eleven, their mother died. In 1865, their forty-two-year-old father married Abby Durfee Gray, thirty-seven. Although Abby was apparently kind to the girls, Emma and Lizzie were not fond of her.

Andrew Borden raised his family in Fall River, Massachusetts, near where his English ancestors had settled in 1638. For

> Lizzie Borden took an ax/ And gave her mother forty whacks/ When she saw what she had done/ She gave her father forty-one.
>
> --Anonymous

11

eight generations the Borden family had been prominent citizens of that community. Working first as an undertaker, Borden ventured into real estate and banking, and eventually built up a fortune. President of the Fall River Savings Bank and senior partner in Borden, Almy, and Company, he owned several textile mills and other real estate. His wealth in 1891 was estimated between \$300,000 and \$500,000. But he was known as a conservative spender who lived very simply. The Borden home was at 92 Second Street, in an unfashionable section of town. The house, a plain two-story frame structure, had no modern plumbing. The interior had no hallways leaving each room opened to another, so that family members enjoyed little or no privacy.

HOME, NOT SO SWEET HOME

"As a child she [Lizzie Borden] was of a very sensitive nature, inclined to be non-communicative with new acquaintances," a contemporary *Boston Herald* article reported, "and this characteristic has tenaciously [stubbornly] clung to her all through life." Lizzie Borden attended high school but she was not a gifted student. "As a scholar she was not remarkable for brilliancy," the *Herald* further noted, "but she was conscientious in her studies and with application always held a good rank in her class."

After graduating from public high school, Borden became heavily involved in the Central Congregational Church. She served as the secretary-treasurer of the Christian Endeavor Society and taught Sunday school. She was also active in the Christian Women's Temperance Union, a group that worked to outlaw alcoholic beverages, as well as the Fruit and Flower League, an organization that cared for the needy. Neither she nor her sister Emma ever married and both continued to live in their father and stepmother's home.

According to reports, the mood in the Borden household was tense and guarded. Around 1884, when Andrew Borden transferred some of his property to his wife (for use by her half-sister), his daughters grew increasingly resentful toward their stepmother. They began to address her as "Mrs. Borden," rather than "Mother," and they demanded an equal share of their father's

wealth. In 1887 Andrew gave his daughters some stocks and bonds, as well as the original family home, which they rented out.

But tensions continued to mount among the Bordens. Family members began to lock themselves in their bedrooms at night. In 1891 an unknown thief stole jewelry and money from the master bedroom. The Bordens responded by changing the locks on the bedroom doors.

A GRUESOME SIGHT

In late July 1892 Lizzie and Emma went to visit out-of-town relatives. Lizzie returned early. Sometime after dinner on August 3, Mr. and Mrs. Borden and their Irish-born housekeeper, Bridget Sullivan, became ill. Abby Borden suspected that someone had tried to poison them.

Tourists can now visit the Borden family home and see the exact room, pictured above, where Andrew Borden was murdered. *Reproduced by permission of AP/Wide World Photos.*

Murder Most Foul

The day of the murders, the *Boston Advertiser* published a story titled "Murder Most Foul. Andrew Borden and his wife killed by an assassin who leaves no clew [clue] to the awful deed." The story begins:

An aged man and his aged wife were killed today, their heads chopped to pieces by repeated and fiendish blows with an axe, the murderer and the implement of slaughter both disappeared, and now, twelve hours after the bloody deed, the police and the people are in just as utter ignorance as they were when it was first noised about this noon.

On Thursday, August 4, at 9:20 a.m., Andrew Borden left for his office. Mrs. Borden, Lizzie, and Bridget remained at home. A neighbor observed Bridget Sullivan walking around the house with a bucket of water to wash windows. At about 10:40 a.m., Mr. Borden returned home, as he usually did, to read his mail and eat his midday meal. Shortly after he returned home, the neighbor who had seen the housekeeper preparing to wash the windows saw Lizzie standing motionless in the side doorway. Lizzie claimed that someone had killed her father and she instructed the neighbor to call the police.

When police arrived at the Borden home, they found Mr. Borden slumped on a blood-stained sofa in the living room. It was a gruesome sight. His head was gashed, a tooth had been split, and one of his eye sockets had been destroyed. Upstairs, in a guest bedroom, the police found the lifeless body of Abby Borden. She, too, had been struck multiple times with a sharp object. She was nearly beheaded.

After medical examinations of the bodies were performed, doctors concluded that both victims had been struck repeatedly with a sharp weapon, such as an ax or hatchet. Andrew Borden had received nine blows; Abby Borden had been struck seventeen times. The doctors also judged that Abby had died one to two hours before her husband was slain. If that timeline was accurate, the killer must have been in or around the Borden house between the two attacks. Yet the killer did not attack Lizzie or Bridget, both of whom were home at that time.

CIRCUMSTANTIAL EVIDENCE

The double murder drew national publicity and people from all over the country wrote to the police with theories and

A Poisonous Accusation

On August 5, 1892, the *Boston Daily Globe* (cited in *The Lizzie Borden Sourcebook*) published news of damning evidence against Lizzie Borden.

"Discovery! A woman inquired for poison. Said that drug clerk identified her. Strange story told by Lizzie Borden."

At D.R. Smith's drug store officials got the first important evidence. They approached the clerk, Eli Bence, and from him learned that Miss [Lizzie] Borden had been in the store within 36 hours past and had inquired for a certain poison. The clerk was asked to accompany the officers and closely questioned as to the exact facts relative to the time, the girl's condition mentally, the amount and quantity of the poison she had bought, or called for.

The officers then led the drug clerk to a residence on 2d. St. where Miss Lizzie was stopping for the time being. The young man was not previously well acquainted with the young woman, but he told them that he could identify her at sight. He did identify her, and in the presence of the police officers informed them that she was in his place of business and made inquiry for a bottle of poison.

suggestions. The Fall River police followed dozens of leads, but none pointed to a suspect. But circumstantial evidence (evidence or conclusions drawn from the situation) pointed to one person: Lizzie Borden, who claimed to have been in the barn looking for fishing sinkers when the murders occurred.

Borden, whose parents had just been killed, was strangely calm when police arrived—whereas the housekeeper, Bridget Sullivan, was hysterical. The apparent delay between killings led police to believe that someone within the household had committed the murders. There was no sign of struggle or forced entry, convincing officials that someone in the household was responsible. And strangely, a woman fitting Borden's description had attempted to buy poison from a druggist shortly before the killings.

Hiram Harrington, Lizzie's uncle, did little to defend his niece. He told the press that both girls, and Lizzie in particular, argued with their father about money. He said that Lizzie sometimes refused to talk to her father for days, and he stated flatly that money had been the motive for the murders. One week

Who Died First?

Doctors who examined the bodies of Abby and Andrew Borden concluded that Mrs. Borden had died an hour or two before her husband. The timing of these killings cast further suspicion on Andrew's daughter Lizzie, who stood to inherit half of the family's valuable estate. Had Andrew Borden died before his wife—even if only by minutes—she would have been named as his heir. And with her death, much of the Borden estate would have passed to her family.

Today historians question whether nineteenth-century doctors were capable of accurately determining time of death. In that era, doctors looked at blood clotting and drying, and analyzed the contents of the victim's stomach to determine the time of death. These processes involve many variables that make it very difficult to pinpoint the time of death.

after the killings, police arrested Lizzie Borden and charged her with the double homicide.

VERDICT: NOT FIENDISH

The August 11 edition of the *New York Herald* (cited in *The Lizzie Borden Sourcebook*) described Lizzie's arrest:

The wonderful courage and self-possession that have sustained this extraordinary woman abandoned her in her chief hour of need. Very likely she had not been without some expectation that possibly such a fate was in store for her, yet at the reading of the warrant she fell into a fit of abject and pitiable terror. A fit of violent trembling seized her, and so complete was the collapse of her physical system, weakened, no doubt, by the prolonged and terrible strain, that instead of the cell that had been prepared for her the matron's room in the central station was made her prison.

Borden remained in prison for nearly a year while the prosecution struggled to build a case against her. They found no solid evidence to prove she had committed the crimes. No murder weapon was found; Borden had not confessed; and no witness came forward to accuse her. Further, a search of Borden's closet had produced no bloody clothing—and she had appeared spotless at the bloody murder scene.

The trial finally began on June 5, 1893, in the Massachusetts Supreme Court. Borden did not take the stand. The prosecution presented a strong case, including testimony from a Harvard chemist who had determined that the dimensions of a hatchet head that had been found in the Borden's basement matched those of the victim's cuts. Borden remained calm throughout the trial. Her defense attorney, who intentionally played up the violent nature of the crimes, posed a question to the jurors in his final argument: "To find her guilty, you must believe she is a fiend. Gentlemen, does she look it?" On June 20, the jury returned after just one hour of deliberation. The verdict: not guilty.

After she was cleared of the murder charges, Lizzie Borden moved with her sister to Maplecroft, a mansion they purchased in a fashionable section of Fall River. When Emma Borden moved out in 1913, Lizzie stayed at Maplecroft alone with her pets. She died of pneumonia in 1927 at the age of sixty-six. Ten days later, her sister, Emma died. Both left a large part of their fortunes to the Animal Rescue League and other charities.

For More Information

Aiuto, Russell. "Lizzie Borden." *The Crime Library.* http://www. crimelibrary.com/lizzie/lizziemain.htm (accessed on August 2, 2002).

Gaute, J. H. H., and Robin Odell. *The New Murderers' Who's Who.* London: Harrap Books Ltd., 1979, 1989, pp. 56–57.

Gottesman, Ronald, ed. *Violence in America: An Encyclopedia.* New York: Charles Scribner's Sons, 1999, vol. 1: pp. 164–166.

James, Edward T., ed. *Notable American Women, 1607–1950: A Biographical Dictionary.* Cambridge, MA: Belknap Press of Harvard University Press, 1971, vol. 1: pp. 210–212.

Kent, David, ed., with Robert A. Flynn. *The Lizzie Borden Sourcebook.* Boston: Branden Publishing Co., 1992.

Macdonald, Lewis. *One Hundred Years of Lizzie Borden.* Contemporary Review (1992), pp. 261, 323+.

Sifakis, Carl. *The Encyclopedia of American Crime.* 2d ed. New York: Facts on File, 2001, vol. 1: pp. 113–114.

Spiering, Frank. *Lizzie.* New York: Random House, 1984.

Christopher Boyce

1953
AKA: The Falcon

Andrew Daulton Lee

1952
AKA: The Snowman
Spies

"Painting is like a sponge. It absorbs all the hurt and passion in life and leaves me healed for the next day."

—Christopher Boyce, quoted in the *Los Angeles Times,* after he was granted parole

Christopher Boyce. *Reproduced by permission of Corbis Corporation.*

Christopher Boyce and Andrew Daulton Lee grew up in a well-to-do suburb in southern California. As young men both were displeased with the United States government. In 1974 Boyce went to work at TRW Systems, an aerospace firm that worked on many classified military programs. In the following years, he smuggled information out of TRW, which Lee then passed to Soviet agents. In 1977 Lee was picked up by police outside the Soviet Embassy in Mexico. The young American was carrying microfilm of documents. The police soon concluded that he was a spy. Lee informed on Boyce, who was picked up ten days later in Los Angeles, California. Both were tried and convicted under the United States Espionage Act. While both received long sentences, Boyce drew additional time after he escaped from prison and robbed a series of banks. **(See original entry on Boyce and Lee in *Outlaws, Mobsters, & Crooks,* Volume 2.)**

GOOD BEHAVIOR

Unlike his partner in espionage, Lee created little trouble as an inmate. Sentenced to life in prison, his good behavior earned

him parole in January 1998. After his release from prison, he went to work at a Hollywood production company owned by Sean Penn—the actor who portrayed him in the 1985 movie *The Falcon and the Snowman*.

Boyce, meanwhile, was not scheduled to be released until the year 2046. Originally sentenced to forty years in prison, he was given another twenty-eight years for his prison break and armed robberies. Boyce read extensively while in prison, and earned a college degree in art and history. Then he went to work on a master's degree in fine arts and creative writing. Working with the FBI, he produced an educational video aimed at teaching army recruits about the consequences of spying. And in 1985 he testified before Congress in Washington, D.C., to help government officials tighten security in intelligence operations.

Sean Penn, left, and Timothy Hutton played Boyce and Lee in the 1985 movie *The Falcon and the Snowman*, named after the spies' code names. *Reproduced by permission of The Kobal Collection.*

TIME OFF

Good behavior did not spare him from the day-to-day realities of prison life. "In federal custody," he wrote, "nature seems reduced to cockroaches, ants and flies." In the federal penitentiary in Marion, Illinois, he was held in solitary confinement for six years. "Almost every day was exactly like the previous," he wrote about that time. "I felt as if I were submerged, alone, in a submarine." He was beaten by a white supremacist gang while in Leavenworth, Kansas, penitentiary. In state prison in Oak Park Heights, Minnesota, he was stalked by an inmate who plotted to kill him. After writing an unpopular opinion piece for a local newspaper, he was given solitary confinement, and then transferred to Supermax in Florence, Colorado. Widely considered to be the federal government's toughest prison, Supermax houses prison gang-leaders and killers such as Unabomber **Ted Kaszynski** (see entry in volume 4) and terrorist **Timothy McVeigh** (see entry).

In 1997 the light appeared at the end of the tunnel when prison officials met to decide whether Boyce would be granted parole. During that meeting, the onetime spy broke down in tears. In the end, the parole commission shared the opinion of Kenneth Walker, a parole commission examiner, who concluded that "Mr. Boyce seems to be a mature individual and one who is truly sorry for his past crimes." The parole examiners recommended that Boyce be released to a halfway house in September 2002. They further concluded that he should be granted a full release in March 2003.

For More Information

"An Inmate Learns That Commentary on Prison Life Can Cost Him." *Star Tribune* (February 15, 1998): p. 25A.

"Boyce and Pollard." *Los Angeles Times* (July 19, 1998): p. 3.

"'Falcon' May Fly Free Again." *Los Angeles Times* (July 10, 1998): p. 1.

"Secrets for Sale." *New York Times* (April 2, 2001): p. 24.

James Bulger

September 3, 1929

AKA: Whitey, Mark Shapeton, Thomas F. Baxter, Tom Harris, Tom Marshall

Mobster

For years James J. Bulger kept Federal Bureau of Investigation (FBI) agents abreast of his Italian enemies' criminal activities in exchange for protection and immunity (charges could not be brought against him). Since his disappearance in 1995, the FBI has undergone internal investigations for its special treatment of informants. More than seventy years old, Bulger is the oldest fugitive on the FBI's Ten Most Wanted Fugitives list.

TOP DOG IN WINTER HILL

As a young man in the Irish-dominated area of South Boston, Massachusetts, James "Whitey" Bulger developed a reputation as a fierce rival. Running with a local Irish gang called the Shamrocks, he soon became involved in serious crimes. He was first arrested at the age of seventeen.

Sometime in the late 1950s, Bulger joined the Winter Hill gang, considered by many to be the Irish equivalent of Boston's Mafia (Italian organized crime). Convicted of bank robbery in 1956, he drew a nine-year sentence at Alcatraz, a federal prison

"Informers would trade their mothers to stay out of jail."

--Boston Globe reporter Kevin Cullen, who wrote a story revealing that Bulger was a government informant

in San Francisco, California. Released from "The Rock," as Alcatraz was known, in 1965, he returned to South Boston and to a life of crime. He moved quickly through the ranks of the Winter Hill gang and, by 1979, had become the leader of that organization (after the previous leader had been shot to death). As the top man in the Winter Hill gang, Bulger oversaw the gang's drug trafficking, gambling, protection, and loan-sharking activities. Fellow mobster Stephen "The Rifleman" Flemmi was considered to be his right-hand man.

In January 1995, a federal grand jury in Boston formally charged Bulger and five others with racketeering (threatening a business for profit) and extortion (using intimidation to force payment). Five days before the grand jury made its decision, Bulger disappeared. It was not the first time Bulger had managed to stay a step ahead of law enforcement officials. In 1981 Massachusetts State Police installed a court-approved wire tap in Bulger's garage office. He immediately stopped using that office to conduct his mob business. When the police planted listening devices in Bulger's car and in pay phones he often used, the same thing happened. The mobster seemed to know that he was being watched. Timothy M. Burke, the former assistant district attorney in Suffolk County (the county Boston lies in) tried to gather evidence against Bulger. He later said to the *New York Times,* "It was clear to us that our efforts were being compromised." Soon, it would become apparent that there was much more to the story of Whitey Bulger than met the eye.

MOLES IN THE MOB

Information provided by Steve Flemmi blew the Bulger case wide open. Flemmi was charged with racketeering, money laundering, loan-sharking (lending money at very high rates of interest), witness tampering, and murder. Unlike Bulger, Flemmi had not managed to pull off a disappearing act. Further, he had an interesting story to tell authorities. In 1997, he surprised everyone, including his own lawyer, when he announced that both he and Bulger had been FBI informants. The government, Flemmi claimed, had approved their crimes in order to gain critical inside information that would help destroy the Boston arm of the Mafia.

Flemmi claimed that his association with the FBI had begun in the 1960s, when Boston was in the midst of gang warfare. Convinced that the Mafia posed a serious threat to national security, high-level federal agents were determined to break up the mob's stronghold in New England. To do this, they enlisted the aid of highly placed informants called TEs, short for Top Echelon (top-level) criminals, who could provide information about gang activities. "In exchange for the information they provide the bureau [FBI]," *New York Times* reporter Carey Goldberg wrote, such confidential informers "are allowed to commit certain crimes and [are] promised the agency's protection if other law-enforcement branches come after them." According to Flemmi, an FBI contact gave the two mobsters license to do anything short of murder: "You can do whatever you want," the agent reportedly told Flemmi and Bulger, "as long as you don't clip [shoot] someone."

Mobster Stephen "The Rifleman" Flemmi, right, testifies how FBI agents recruited him, much like they recruited Bulger, as an informant and protected him from being indicted for over twenty-five years. *Reproduced by permission of AP/Wide World Photos.*

MUTUAL BACK-SCRATCHING

At first, the FBI denied any involvement with Flemmi and Bulger. That denial soon gave way to the admission that there was a close relationship between certain FBI agents and criminal informants. Eventually the details of Bulger's role as an informant emerged. In 1975 John Connolly, an FBI agent who was considered to be a rising star, had approached Bulger to propose an arrangement.

Their first meeting took place at midnight, at a beach just outside of South Boston. That meeting cemented an arrangement that would last for two decades, from 1975 to 1995. Bulger provided the FBI with critical information about his competition—the Boston arm of the Mafia. In exchange, Connolly provided the mobster with information that allowed him to avoid arrest. Further, it is possible that Connolly provided Bulger with information about informants within the mobster's own organization. In 1976 an FBI informant was killed—allegedly in response to a tip from Connolly.

Connolly's arrangement with Bulger set off a heated debate about FBI policy and the agency's use of informants. Some believed that Connolly was simply a maverick agent whose actions were not supported by the FBI. Others claimed that Connolly acted with the full support of the agency, and that such arrangements were common. Critics began questioning the bureau's ethical standards. Responding to these issues, the FBI conducted far-reaching internal investigations and the U.S. Justice Department launched a massive policy review.

HOW BAD ARE THE BAD GUYS?

Acting on tips from the Irish mobsters, federal agents were able to land convictions and jail terms for a long list of Mafia members. As a result, the Boston arm of Italian organized crime was virtually destroyed.

FBI agent Connolly later described his agreement with Bulger and Flemmi as a practical trade-off in which the end justified the means. "It was a business decision, pure and simple," he told the *New York Times*. "We were going to use a gang of two to get rid of a gang of 42.... The 42 people we put away were probably responsible for 200 murders over 30 years, maybe more."

Pros and Cons

"You're always weighing how bad are the bad guys versus how good is the information they're providing. That's the dilemma." --Robert M. Bloom, professor of law and specialist in federal procedure at Boston College Law School, quoted in the *New York Times*

Defense attorneys, too, argue that the mobsters' actions were justified and should not be prosecuted. Flemmi's lawyers claimed that he had been promised protection from prosecution, but their claim was denied. The mobsters' attorneys also questioned whether racketeering laws apply when a criminal is working for the government. "If people like Whitey Bulger were cooperating with the government," attorney Elliot Weinstein argued, "then it may well be that the defendants did not have the necessary criminal intent to be part of a conspiracy, because they were actually acting at the behest [order] of the government."

Ethics 101

Bulger's role as a FBI informant prompted the agency to reconsider its policies and establish new procedures. After reviewing the guidelines for using informants, FBI officials began to require ethics training for first-time informants. As for the ethical conduct of agents, the behavioral science arm of the bureau attempted to screen prospective agents to determine whether they are inclined to make unethical decisions.

EQUAL OPPORTUNITY MURDER

As more informants came forward, Bulger's criminal career came into sharper focus. Initially considered to be a mobster who avoided violence, Bulger was eventually named as a participant in a series of homicides. It is believed that the Bulger group committed more than twenty murders in as many years—ranging from Boston to Florida and Oklahoma. In September 2000, Bulger—who was still a fugitive—was indicted (formally charged) by a federal grand jury for his involvement in eighteen murders, many of which were committed during his years as an FBI informant. Flemmi was indicted for his role in ten murders.

The indictments outlined the murders in gory detail. Among the victims were rivals, longtime associates, friends, lovers, as well as certain individuals who happened to be "in the wrong place at the wrong time." Roger Wheeler, a distinguished businessman from Oklahoma, was murdered in 1981 as Bulger associates attempted to take over his business. Flemmi's and Bulger's girlfriends were killed because they knew too much. Rivals were eliminated. Informants were silenced. And potential witnesses were dealt with in the same way. Some of the murders were motivated by revenge—and some were outright mistakes.

AN AGING BONNIE AND CLYDE

On the run since 1995, Bulger has managed to travel around the country with his younger girlfriend, Catherine

The Other Bulger

"Whitey" Bulger's brother, William M. Bulger, followed an entirely different career path. He served as president of the Massachusetts state senate for eighteen years and in 1996 became president of the prestigious University of Massachusetts. Interestingly, reporters have noted that John Connolly, "Whitey" Bulger's FBI contact, acted as a volunteer in Senator Bulger's election campaign. William Bugler has never been accused of any involvement in his brother's crimes.

Grieg, without attracting attention. "Like Bonnie and Clyde on Geritol—or in his case, the heart medication Atenolol—Whitey and Catherine stay on the move," wrote *Gazette-Mail* reporter Larry McShane. A fit, white-haired man who wears glasses and a baseball cap, he looks like a harmless elderly man, although he reportedly always carries a knife. "The once-feared gangster looks more grandfather than godfather, just another anonymous senior citizen," said McShane.

The Bulger case has been mentioned many times on television's *America's Most Wanted* and *Unsolved Mysteries* programs. But few genuine clues have resulted. His whereabouts remain unknown. Bulger has been spotted in New York, Louisiana, Florida, California, Iowa, Wyoming, and Mississippi. The oldest criminal on the FBI's Ten Most Wanted list, there is a $1-million reward for his capture.

Federal agents once tracked Bulger to Grande Isle, Louisiana. But Bulger was long gone. Henry Wellman, who was the mobster's landlord for six weeks, was shocked to hear that his tenant was a wanted man. Wellman described Bulger as "just an elderly guy with his wife, the grandfather type. A nice guy, he stayed to himself."

Authorities believe that Bulger owes his success as a fugitive to foresight. In the years preceding his disappearance, the mobster stashed money in safety deposit boxes around the country. With the money he is able to withdraw from banks under false identities, he can live comfortably without leaving the paper trail that most bank transactions create.

For More Information

America's Most Wanted. http://www2.amw.com/amw.html (accessed on July 26, 2002).

Butterfield, Fox. "New England Crime Bosses Could Appeal." *New York Times* (June 16, 1997): National Desk.

Goldberg, Carey. "2000 Campaign: A Debate Backdrop; It's Where the Bodies Are." *New York Times* (September 22, 2000): National Desk.

Goldberg, Carey. "Boston Fugitive, Associate Indicted in Several Murders; 18 Slayings Are Linked to Reputed Mob Boss." *Washington Post* (September 29, 2000): Section A.

Goldberg, Carey. "Boston Trial's Troublesome Crux: How to Handle Informers' Crimes." *New York Times* (March 13, 1999): National Desk.

Goldberg, Carey. "Court Ruling Sets Guides on Use of Informers." *New York Times* (September 16, 1999): National Desk.

Goldberg, Carey. "Once-Shielded Mob Figure Is Charged by U.S. in Murders." *New York Times* (September 29, 2000): National Desk.

Lehr, Dick, and Gerard O'Neill. *Black Mass: The Irish Mob, the FBI, and a Devil's Deal.* New York: Public Affairs, 2000.

Marcus, Jon. "Setting Up Mobsters in the Press?" *American Journalism Review* 21 (December 1999): pp. 14–15.

McShane, Larry. "Bonnie, Clyde and Geritol: Mobster, Moll Still Running." *Gazette-Mail (Charleston, West Virginia)* (March 25, 2001).

Dalton Gang

(Grattan Dalton)
(Robert Dalton)
(Emmet Dalton)

Robbers and Bandits

"What had begun as an ordinary, peaceful day in a small town on the southeastern border of Kansas had turned into a nightmare that would haunt the townspeople for years."

--Rosemary Davis, writing for *American History*

Grattan Dalton.

Grattan, Robert, and Emmet Dalton were experienced horse thieves and bank robbers. In trying to outdo their second cousins, Bob and Cole Younger of the infamous Jesse James gang, the Daltons staged two bank robberies at the same time in their former hometown.

FIFTEEN FATHERLESS FRONTIER KIDS

Abandoned by their father, Lewis Dalton, the fifteen Dalton children were raised by their mother, Adeline Younger Dalton, a devout Sunday-school teacher. Raised in a frontier region that now forms the border between Kansas and Missouri, they experienced the tensions brought on by the Civil War (1861–65) and Reconstruction (the period of rebuilding that followed the Civil War). The family moved several times in a short span of time, pulling up stakes in Montgomery, Kansas (near Coffeyville), to settle on a farm in Missouri, and later moving to the Cherokee Nation, in what is now Oklahoma.

Of the large brood of Dalton children, three died in youth and seven (three girls and four boys) became law-abiding citizens.

Ben, the oldest boy, remained with his mother, while three others took up farming in California. Franklin Dalton became a United States deputy marshal in 1884. Three years later, at the age of twenty-eight, he was killed while trying to arrest bootleggers.

The remaining brothers, all reportedly clean-cut, handsome, and polite, turned to crime. Grattan ("Grat"; 1861–1892), Robert (1870–1892), and Emmet (1871–1937) Dalton formed the core of what became known as the Dalton gang. Their brother Bill later struck out on his own in an unsuccessful attempt to lead a life of crime.

The Other Infamous Dalton

Bill Dalton did not take part in the Coffeyville raid. After his brothers were killed or jailed, he joined Bill Doolin's gang, and later, in 1894, formed his own gang. With just one botched bank robbery to his gang's credit, Bill fled from Texas to Oklahoma. On June 8, 1894, he was killed as he attempted to escape from law officers.

PLAYING BOTH SIDES OF THE LAW

After Franklin was killed in the line of duty, Grat and Robert joined the federal marshals—possibly intending to avenge their brother's death. Although Emmet, the youngest brother, was too young to enlist as a U.S. marshal, he rode with his two older siblings. By 1890 Grat and Robert, who apparently did not strictly follow the law, were dismissed as marshals. According to some sources, they were fired for stealing horses. Other accounts report that the Daltons learned too much about a gambling organization and were dismissed by the influential men who organized the ring.

Grattan set out for California, where his brother Bill had settled. Meanwhile, Robert and Emmet joined forces with a number of other outlaws, including George Newcomb, Charley Bryant, and Bill McElhanie. The gang rustled horses and cattle, and, after landing in Silver City, New Mexico, robbed a gambling establishment. As the gang's reputation grew, they found it increasingly difficult to hide from the law officers who hunted them. Eventually Robert and Emmet joined their brothers in California.

GUN FIGHTS AND TRAIN HEISTS

On February 6, 1891, Emmet, Grattan, and Robert reportedly attempted to rob a Southern Pacific train. When the express messenger resisted, a gun fight broke out and the train's fireman was wounded and died. The brothers split up and Grat-

Emmet Dalton, the youngest of the Dalton brothers, was the only to survive a bloody shootout with law officers, receiving sixteen bullet wounds.

tan was arrested with his brother Bill, who had no part in the robbery. After his arrival in California, Bill Dalton had launched a promising political career. Although he was cleared of any charges of involvement in his brothers' attempted train robbery, his hopes of becoming a major player in California's political arena were now dashed.

The charges against Grattan stuck. Although there was no solid evidence tying him to the crime, he was convicted and sentenced to serve twenty years in California's San Quentin prison. But he served barely any time there. In September, almost immediately after his conviction, he escaped from jail and rejoined his brothers in Oklahoma.

In the following months, the Dalton gang robbed banks and trains throughout an area that stretched from Oklahoma to Arkansas and Kansas to Texas. On September 15, now joined by Bill Doolin (a friend and fellow robber), the gang robbed the Missouri, Kansas, and Texas train of several thousand dollars. (Emmet Dalton later reported that their haul was $19,000, but this figure is widely questioned.)

The Daltons then staged a daring holdup in Red Rock, Arkansas, and then continued in other states. They did not meet with armed resistance until they struck the Katy Railroad. On July 14, 1892, as the Katy train pulled into Adair, in eastern Oklahoma, the Dalton gang encountered thirteen armed guards who had been hired to protect the train. After a fifteen-minute shoot-out, one civilian was dead and a handful of officers and a civilian had been wounded. None of the robbers had been touched. Although papers reported that the bandits had made off with $70,000, the actual figure is probably closer to $10,000.

A ROBBERY RUN AWRY

The Dalton brothers were second cousins of Bob and Cole Younger, who belonged to the **Jesse James** gang (see entry in volume 3). Having enjoyed modest success as bank and train robbers, the Daltons reportedly decided to outdo their notorious relatives. They planned to rob not one but two banks, in broad daylight, in their hometown of Coffeyville, Kansas. This caper would be their last.

On October 5, 1892, Robert, Grat, and Emmet rode into Coffeyville with Dick Broadwell (also known as Texas Jack) and Bill Powers (also known as Tom Evans). Bill Doolin did not go with them. Although many accounts claim that the Daltons wore fake beards to disguise their identity, Emmet later claimed that they did no such thing. The men were heavily armed.

From the start, the robbery did not go as planned. The hitches where they intended to tie their horses had been removed because of construction, forcing the bandits to leave their horses in an alley that led into the town square. As the gang made their way to the two banks, grocer Aleck McKenna recognized one of the Daltons—supposedly because of his unusual way of walking. As three of the robbers entered the C. M. Condon & Company Bank and the other two positioned themselves in the First National Bank, McKenna alerted the townspeople that the Daltons were up to something.

Robert Dalton, a former U.S. marshal, joined his brothers robbing trains and banks and was later killed in a bloody shoot-out with the townspeople of Coffeyville.

Because both banks had large glass windows in front, some townspeople were able to witness the robberies. Martin Davenport, who was driving a delivery wagon, charged his horses through the main street shouting the news about the crimes in progress. Soon, the town was up in arms. Citizens crowded into the town's two hardware stores—A. P. Boswell & Company and Ishum Brothers & Mansur—where they were given firearms and ammunition. They then positioned themselves behind old metal stoves in front of the stores, which happened to be in the line of the bandits' escape route.

In what was later described as "the bloodiest fifteen minutes in the history of American outlawry" eight of the robbers were killed and four were wounded. Of the outlaws, only Emmet Dalton survived. He received sixteen bullet wounds, and was later tried and convicted of armed robbery. Sentenced to a

Bill Doolin--"King of Oklahoma Outlaws"

Born in 1858, Bill Doolin worked on his family's farm and often practiced shooting, soon becoming an expert marksman. In 1881, at age twenty-three, Doolin decided to head west to take advantage of the opportunities the frontier promised. Working for Oscar D. Halsell at the H.H. Ranch, he got to know a number of cowboys who would later become outlaws, including Emmet Dalton. (In fact, most of the outlaws who would later make up the Dalton and Doolin gangs had once worked at the H.H. Ranch.)

Eventually Doolin, who was known as an honest man, wound up on the wrong side of the law. As part of the Dalton gang, he participated in one of their first train robberies, at Red Rock, Arkansas. Considered to be an extremely quick and accurate shooter, he took part in a number of other train robberies as a member of that gang. But on October 5, 1892, when the Dalton gang launched their attack on two Coffeyville banks, Doolin was absent.

According to some accounts, Doolin was originally part of the raiding party, until his horse became lame. Others claim that he had already been voted out of the gang by the time the heist was planned. Still others note that Doolin might have declined to participate because he considered the risks of the Coffeyville raid to be too high.

life term, he served only fourteen years in the Kansas State Prison. The former outlaw, who found religion while doing time in the state prison, was granted a full pardon by President Theodore Roosevelt (1858–1919).

For More Information

Dalton, Robert. "The Only Outlaw to Survive the Raid on Coffeyville, Emmet Dalton Went to Jail and to Hollywood." *Wild West* (August 2001): p. 12.

Dalton Gang. http://www.daltongang.com/ (accessed on August 2, 2002).

Davis, Rosemary. "The Day the Daltons Rode into Town." *American History* (September/October 1992): p. 44.

Drago, Harry Sinclair. *Road Agents and Train Robbers.* New York: Dodd, Mead & Company, 1973.

Hanes, Colonel Bailey C. *Bill Doolin Outlaw O.T.* Norman, OK: University of Oklahoma Press, 1968.

Soon Doolin put together his own gang. Quiet, soft spoken, and level-headed, he had a gift for leadership and a talent for planning. While the Dalton gang's reign lasted just over one year, the Doolin gang was active over the course of four years—thanks, in great part, to Doolin's leadership. The onetime farmer and cowboy eventually became known as the "king of Oklahoma outlaws."

Doolin apparently tried to avoid violence when possible, but he was known to kill in self defense. Nevertheless, his life came to a violent end. According to reports, Doolin, who had tired of the outlaw life, planned to settle down as a law-abiding citizen with his family. But with a $5,000 reward posted for his capture—dead or alive—Doolin was a wanted man. In August 1896, a posse of marshals ambushed him in Payne County, in the Territory of Oklahoma. Shot in the chest, he died at the scene. An examination of the body revealed that over the course of his short life Doolin had received twenty-one wounds above the waist and a bullet lodged in his head.

Rasmussen, Cecilia. "Los Angeles; L.A. Then and Now; Outlaw Emmet Dalton Went from Guns to Religion to Show Biz." *Los Angeles Times* (July 5, 2001): p. B-4.

Roberts, Gary L. *The New Encyclopedia of the American West.* New Haven, CT: Yale University Press, 1988, pp. 284–285.

Byron de la Beckwith

1920

January 2001

Murderer

On the evening of June 12, 1963, Byron de la Beckwith shot and killed Medgar Evers (1925–1963), the Mississippi field secretary for the National Association for the Advancement of Colored People (NAACP). Remarkably, it took three trials and more than thirty years for a jury to convict Beckwith of the murder. Upon his conviction, civil rights activists expressed relief, but the defense questioned whether Beckwith's right to a speedy trial had been upheld.

RAISED AS A RACIST

Born in Colusa, California, Beckwith lost his father when he was just six years old. A troubled alcoholic, Byron de la Beckwith Sr. died of pneumonia "with contributory alcoholism," according to his death certificate. He left his wife, Susie Yerger Beckwith, with staggering debts and no means to support her only child. The two moved to Greenwood, Mississippi, where her parents, Lemuel and Susie Yerger, took them into their home. Raised in the tradition of a Mississippi plantation, Beckwith learned the rituals of southern courtesy, but also learned racist beliefs.

In Greenwood, African Americans lived in a neighborhood referred to as "Niggertown" by white people. Throughout the South, Jim Crow (segregation) laws separated whites from blacks in public places. From restaurants to restrooms, blacks were relegated to separate and unequal facilities. Lynchings (violent attacks on black victims by white mobs) were not uncommon.

Before the Civil War (1861–65), the Yerger plantation had relied on black slaves to operate. In young Beckwith's day the few black workers on the property were treated with little respect. He learned from his relatives and neighbors to regard African Americans as inferior, derisively calling them "mud people." He addressed black men as "boy." And he considered it his Christian duty to avoid racial integration.

SOLDIERS IN THE FAMILY

By the time Beckwith was twelve, both his grandparents had died. His grandfather, who had fought for the South during the Civil War, was laid to rest in his Confederate uniform. The following year, Beckwith's mother died. She had suffered from emotional problems since the death of her husband, was stricken with inoperable colon cancer, and was unable to eat. Her death certificate listed starvation as a contributing cause of death.

Thirteen years old at the time his mother died, Beckwith moved in with two older, unmarried uncles. At nineteen he graduated from public high school—after having been kicked out of two prep schools, the Webb School and Columbia Military Academy. Next he enrolled at the University of Mississippi. The bombing of Pearl Harbor on December 7, 1941, cut short his college career.

On January 5, 1942, Beckwith joined the U.S. Marine Corps. He fought in the Pacific during World War II (1939–45) and was wounded in the bloody fighting on the island of Tarawa. He returned home a hero and was later awarded the Purple Heart medal, an honor given to American soldiers who are wounded while fighting for their country.

TWO WIVES, FOUR MARRIAGES, AND THREE DIVORCES

After recovering from his wounds, Beckwith completed his military duty stateside. On September 22, 1945, he married

Mary Louise Williams, a WAVE (Women Accepted for Volunteer Emergency Service) he had met while in the service. Honorably discharged from the marines, Beckwith returned with his wife to Greenwood, where he worked as a traveling salesman for a tobacco company.

The honeymoon did not last long. Beckwith—a man who drank to excess and was prone to violence—reportedly abused his wife on many occasions. They were divorced and married three times before Beckwith married his second wife, Thelma.

THE MURDER OF MEDGAR EVERS

Early in his presidency, John F. Kennedy (1917–1963) was openly criticized for not sufficiently involving his administration in the civil rights movement. On June 12, 1963, he delivered a speech declaring his intent to support the cause. That evening, Medgar Evers, the thirty-seven-year-old Mississippi field chairman for the NAACP, watched the president's speech on television at NAACP headquarters in Jackson, Mississippi. His wife and three young children watched the address at their Jackson home. Evers had agreed to allow the two oldest children to stay up until he returned, so they could discuss the president's comments.

Shortly after midnight, Evers pulled into his driveway. Carrying sweatshirts printed with the slogan "Jim Crow Must Go," he got out of the car and turned to walk up his driveway. Before he reached his house, he fell to the ground, having been shot in the back by a high-power deer rifle. The bullet, which left a hole in his back the size of a fifty-cent piece, passed through him and entered the house. A neighbor fired a shot in the air to scare off the assailant, whom no one had seen. Others prepared to take Evers to the hospital. He died shortly thereafter.

Evers had been an outspoken champion of integration and had become a central figure in the hotly contested debate over legal desegregation. To people on both sides of the issue, he represented the civil rights movement. As news of his assassination spread, racial tensions rose throughout the country. In Jackson, Mississippi, the threat of further violence and rioting was unmistakable.

ALIBI VS. EVIDENCE

Police readily recovered the murder weapon. Experts found a fingerprint on the rifle's telescopic sight. That print belonged to Byron de la Beckwith, to whom the gun was registered. But, claiming his gun had been stolen, Beckwith denied any involvement in the killing. He also claimed that he had been in Greenwood, 80 miles (129 kilometers) from Jackson, on the night of the Evers's slaying. Two policemen later confirmed that they had seen Beckwith in Greenwood that night.

But the circumstantial evidence against him was staggering. Other witnesses placed him in Jackson that night. One person had seen a white Plymouth Valiant, like Beckwith's, parked near Evers's house one hour before the shooting. Two cab drivers identified him as a man who had asked for directions to the civil rights leader's house four days before the incident. And Beckwith was clearly tied to the murder weapon.

TWO TRIALS AND NO VERDICT

Beckwith was formally charged in 1963 with the murder of Medgar Evers. Within two days of his arrest, the people of Greenwood established the White Citizens Legal Fund to pay for his legal fees. Through flyers, letters, and articles in southern newspapers, the fund solicited donations and soon raised more than enough to pay for Beckwith's defense.

Beckwith's trial, which began in January 1964, attracted tremendous publicity in the state of Mississippi and throughout the nation. Many expected the defendant, who enjoyed the support of the majority of white Mississippians, to be acquitted (found not guilty). Civil rights activist John Salter later expressed a common opinion: "White men in Mississippi in 1964 simply were not going to convict another white man of shooting a 'trouble-making' Negro like Medgar."

The "Fate of a Patriot"

Awaiting his first trial (in early 1964) for the murder of Medgar Evers in the Hind County jail, Beckwith wrote a letter to his wife. He gave little indication of concern about his situation. He wrote, "As you know this is the first rest I've had in twenty years. I could take all of us to Europe or to Mexico for what this will cost—such is the fate of a patriot."

As the trial got underway, District Attorney William Waller put forth a convincing circumstantial case against Beckwith. Judge Leon Hendrick presided fairly over the proceedings. And yet, after eleven hours of deliberation, the jury reported that it was hopelessly deadlocked. With a split decision of six to six, Judge Hendrick was forced to declare a mistrial. In April 1964 Beckwith was tried again. That jury, too, was deadlocked. Beckwith, who bragged to other segregationists that he had killed Medgar Evers, was released from jail. In 1969 the charge against him was dismissed.

DUE PROCESS AND DOUBLE JEOPARDY

In a strange twist of events, Beckwith was stopped at a police road block in New Orleans, Louisiana in 1973. A search of his car produced a time bomb, various weapons, and a map to the home of a Jewish leader of the Anti-Defamation League of B'Nai Brith. When Detective Ephraim O'Sullivan asked him if he had been arrested before, Beckwith responded, "I shot Medgar Evers." Charged with and convicted of transporting explosives, Beckwith was sentenced to serve time in a Louisiana prison.

Released from prison in 1976, Beckwith's trouble with the law appeared to be behind him. But in 1989, the *Clarion-Ledger,* a Jackson, Mississippi newspaper, revealed that the Mississippi Sovereignty Commission, a staunch segregationist group to which Beckwith belonged, had influenced the jury selection in the second murder trial.

Medgar Evers's widow, Myrlie Evers Williams, asked that the case against Beckwith be reopened. The retrial had the support of the *Clarion-Ledger,* the NAACP, and the Jackson (Mississippi) City Council. Beckwith's supporters argued that he was being denied his constitutional rights. They claimed he was being placed in double jeopardy (tried two times for the same crime) and that he had been denied due process (the right to a speedy trial). But the U.S. Supreme Court reviewed the facts of the case and ruled that a retrial for the 1964 murder was not unconstitutional.

THIRD TIME'S THE CHARM

Tried for the third time in 1994 by a racially mixed jury, Beckwith was convicted of murder and sentenced to life in

Crime-- and Punish- ment?

"He wants to be known as the man who killed Medgar Evers. He just doesn't want to pay for it." --Reed Massengill, Beckwith's nephew, quoted in the *Detroit Free Press*

prison. The seventy-three-year-old, who had worn a Confederate flag lapel pin throughout the proceedings, appeared stunned by the trial's outcome.

The state of Mississippi rejected Beckwith's appeal to have the verdict overturned. Justice Mike Mills wrote, "Miscreants [criminals] brought before the bar of justice in this state must, sooner or later, face the cold realization that justice, slow and plodding though she may be, is certain in the state of Mississippi."

Jackson attorney Merrida Coxwell then drafted an appeal to the Supreme Court. "The lower court sacrificed the petitioner's constitutional rights," he wrote in the appeal, "to atone for Mississippi's past sins." In 1997 that appeal was also denied. Beckwith died at the University of Mississippi Medical Center, at the age of eighty, while serving life in prison.

Myrlie Evers, center, is overcome with emotion after Byron de la Beckwith is found guilty of the murder of her husband, Medgar Evers, almost thirty years after his death. *Reproduced by permission of AP/Wide World Photos.*

For More Information

"Beckwith 'Hopeful' Appeal Will Be Heard." *The (Memphis, TN) Commercial Appeal* (July 1, 1998), p. A5.

Brown, Timothy. "Medgar Evers' Killer Dead at 80; Beckwith Was Convicted in '94 of Murder in '63." *The Charlotte (NC) Observer* (January 23, 2001).

DeLaughter, Bobby. *Never Too Late: A Prosecutor's Story of Justice in the Medgar Evers Case.* New York: Scribner, 2001.

"Idea of Beckwith Pardon 'Absurd,' Fordice Says." *The (Memphis, TN) Commercial Appeal* (September 10, 1999), p. A13.

Layman, Richard, ed. *American Decades: 1960–1969.* Detroit, MI: Gale Research, 1995, pp. 293–294.

Martin, Waldo E., Jr., and Patricia Sullivan, eds. *Civil Rights in the United States.* New York: Macmillan Reference USA, 2000, vol. 1: p. 263–264.

Massengill, Reed. *Portrait of a Racist: The Man Who Killed Medgar Evers?* New York: St. Martin's Press, 1994.

Tucker, Neely. "Unsettled History." *Detroit Free Press* (February 14, 1993), p. 1F.

Vollers, Maryanne. *Ghosts of Mississippi: The Murder of Medgar Evers, The Trials of Byron de la Beckwith, and the Haunting of the New South.* Boston and New York: Little, Brown and Co., 1995.

John Gotti

October 27, 1940
June 10, 2002

AKA: The Teflon Don

Mobster

The Mafia is a secret organization of criminals who may control gambling, drug sales, and other illegal activities in a city or area. The Italian Mafia in the United States is dominated by "families" of criminals who are loyal to one another. Each family is organized like a business, with each person assigned a certain job and one boss, or don, making the decisions and issuing orders. John Gotti rose to the top of the Mafia's Gambino family at a young age. For years he served as a Mafia boss, earning the nickname the Teflon Don because of his ability to make sure that police charges against him did not stick. Arrested several times, he managed to stay out of jail. **(See original entry on Gotti in *Outlaws, Mobsters, & Crooks,* Volume 1.)**

But in 1992 Gotti's high-level hit man (killer for the Mafia), Salvatore "Sammy the Bull" Gravano, volunteered to testify against his boss and other members of the Mafia. This time the charges against Gotti stuck. Convicted of murder and racketeering (threatening a business for profit), Gotti was sentenced to life in prison without possibility of parole (early release). In 1998, just a few years into his life sentence, the former don

"He is suffering from cancer...in an advanced stage. No matter what his physical condition, his mind always works the same."

--Joseph Corozzo, one of Gotti's lawyers, quoted by *Knight/Ridder Tribune News Service*

The Saga of Sammy the Bull

In 1998 mobster Salvatore "Sammy the Bull" Gravano provided testimony, or evidence, that led to the conviction of John Gotti and thirty-six other fellow mobsters. A Mafia hit man who confessed to nineteen murders, Gravano cooperated with officials in exchange for leniency—he disclosed the crimes of his colleagues so that his own punishment would not be as severe. He was sentenced to just five years in prison for his crimes.

Released in 1995, Gravano went into the federal witness protection program. Plastic surgery changed his appearance and he was given a phony birth certificate, marriage license, and social security number. Transplanted to Phoenix, Arizona, he posed as Jimmy Moran, a contractor from South Dakota.

Gravano realized that his former mob colleagues probably knew where he was. "In the mob," he told the press, "anytime anybody flips [reveals Mafia information to law enforcement] there's an open contract on him [to kill him]. I'm not running from the Mafia. I could go to Montana and live twenty years in a cabin and be scared to death. Or I can live here, where I'm happy, for five years."

In Phoenix, the former hit man made little effort to hide his true identity. Eventually, he left the witness protection program. He openly revealed who he was and was happy to give his autograph to those who asked. His book, titled *Underboss: Sammy the Bull Gravano's Story of Life in the Mafia*, included a post-surgery picture of him on the cover. He even appeared on television with

developed throat cancer from which he eventually died from on June 10, 2002.

"I never killed anybody in a fit of rage. Everybody I killed was planned. I'm a hit man, not a serial killer." --Salvatore Gravano, quoted in the *London Times*

JUST ANOTHER BATTLE IN LIFE

When Gotti was fifty-seven years old and had served five years in the federal prison in Marion, Illinois, he was diagnosed with throat cancer. He soon underwent chemotherapy (chemical treatment to fight or control disease) and surgery to remove a tumor from his neck. Many thought that the Mafia don had conquered the cancer. But during a routine checkup in September 2000, doctors discovered that the cancer had returned. This time Gotti was diagnosed with cancer of the neck, head, and throat. The outlook was poor since experts believe that a second series of chemotherapy is generally less successful than the first.

ABC news correspondent Diane Sawyer to promote his book.

Gravano enjoyed the lifestyle of the rich and famous. He and his wife Debra freely spent their money at restaurants and shops. They even paid cash for their cars; each family member drove a high-priced Lexus sedan. "He seemed to own half a Lexus dealership," a neighbor told the *New York Times*.

The Federal Bureau of Investigation (FBI) soon became suspicious of Gravano's lifestyle. His pool construction company had only two jobs on record, which could not have supported his many expenses. Yet the company registered regular payments. Eventually, law enforcement agents were able to charge Gravano as the head of a drug-dealing ring in Arizona and New Mexico. Extradited (surrendered to another legal

authority) from New Mexico, he was charged in New York for possession of forty thousand tablets of the drug known as Ecstasy. Gravano now faces a long prison term.

(Photo of Gravano reproduced by permission of Corbis Corporation.)

Gotti's health worsened after he was transferred to a federal prison hospital in Springfield, Missouri. Chemotherapy had caused him to lose so much weight that doctors decided to discontinue treatment. It was reported that the once-robust mobster withered to only 100 pounds (45 kilograms). "This is just another battle in his life, and he's fighting," Gotti lawyer Joseph Corozzo told the press. Hospital officials required Gotti to use a wheelchair—against his will. "He's forced to be in a wheelchair," Corozzo told the press. But Gotti "insists on getting about on his own without assistance. John is defiant to the end."

THE BEAT GOES ON

Family and friends complained about the treatment Gotti received in the hospital. The former don was reportedly held in a small room behind three sets of doors. They also claimed that doctors and nurses did not visit him often enough. "I'm distressed by the isolation," Corozzo told the press. "His family, his attorneys are all distressed by the isolation. It seems inherently unjust for a terminally ill patient [a patient with no hope of recovery] to be isolated from assistance and human contact."

Corozzo also claimed that the hospital warden, Bill Hedrick—who had been warden at the Marion penitentiary during Gotti's stay there—had singled out the Teflon Don to receive harsh treatment. The ailing mobster was refused contact with his grandchildren, placed in a Plexiglas enclosure to prevent physical contact with his family, and denied commissary privileges (the freedom to purchase food and other supplies from the prison hospital's store). Only one other inmate—Terry Nichols, convicted in the Oklahoma City bombing—has been denied commissary privileges.

By June 2001 doctors reported that Gotti's cancer had worsened and he had only weeks to live. But by August 2001 he had recovered enough to be transferred back to prison. His health situation again declined and Gotti was re-hospitalized for his illness. He died on June 10, 2002 at a federal prison hospital in Springfield, Missouri.

For More Information

"Gotti Reportedly Gravely Ill With Cancer." *Washington Post* (June 13, 2001): p. A16.

"Gravano's Bail Set at $5 Million." *United Press International* (February 28, 2000).

Jerry Capeci's Gang Land. http://www.ganglandnews.com/gotti.htm (accessed August 2, 2002).

"John Gotti." *Maclean's* (October 5, 1998): p. 11.

"John Gotti Jr." *U.S. News & World Report* (February 2, 1998): p. 5.

Smith, Greg B. "Gotti Is Near Death, as Doctors Stop Chemotherapy." *Knight-Ridder/Tribune News Service* (June 13, 2001): p. K5621.

Smith, Greg B. "Prison Doctors Give Crime Boss John Gotti Only Two Months to Live." *Knight-Ridder/Tribune News Service* (April 18, 2001): p. K7622.

"Strip Club's Owner Admits Racketeering; Kaplan, 4 Others Make Deal During Trial." *Washington Post* (August 3, 2001): p. A03.

"Who's Da Boss?" *U.S. News & World Report* (August 28, 2000): p. 8.

An Eerie Similarity

John Gotti's Mafia mentor, Agniello Dellacroce, was being treated for cancer when he died on December 2, 1985.

Charles Keating Jr.

December 4, 1923

Swindler

In the 1980s the U.S. government was deregulating the savings and loan industry, making it comply with fewer federal requirements. At this time Charles Keating purchased Lincoln Savings and Loan (S&L) in Arizona for $51 million. By 1990 he was charged with securities fraud. Instead of carefully guarding depositors' money, he had made high-risk investments that lost millions and caused the failure of the Lincoln S&L. The government stepped in to bail out Lincoln, at an estimated cost of somewhere between $2.5 million and $2.5 billion to U.S. taxpayers. Keating and his family benefited from his Lincoln transactions, as did five U.S. senators (the so-called Keating Five), who received campaign contributions from him. With the help of these high-ranking officials, Keating pressured the Federal Home Loan Bank Board, the regulatory board charged with investigating bank fraud, to ignore his mismanagement. But his investment schemes caught up with him and he was eventually found guilty of fraud.

"Give us our assets back and let us work them out, see what happens."

--Charles Keating, quoted in *Newsmakers*

Decent Literature, Indecent Investments

Charles Keating was born in Cincinnati, Ohio, in 1923. As a young man, he was an accomplished swimmer, winning a gold medal at the 1944 Pan American Games. During World War II (1939–45), he served as Navy fighter pilot, and later enrolled in the University of Cincinnati. Working to put himself through school, he graduated from college and law school in 1948—a feat he accomplished in just two and a half years.

As a young attorney, Keating organized Citizens for Decent Literature, an organization devoted to fighting pornography. He became a founding partner of the Cincinnati law firm Keating, Muething & Klekamp. There he worked with Carl Lindner, head of the American Financial Corporation, a Cincinnati banking and insurance firm. In 1972 Keating became an executive vice president of Lindner's company.

At American Financial, Keating made $50 million for the corporation by using local stockbrokers to sell debentures (bonds backed by the general credit of the issuer rather than on a particular asset) at a high interest rate to individual clients. The company's venture was not underwritten, or guaranteed, by other financial institutions. In other words, American Financial had not insured itself against potential losses. Keating's questionable business practices attracted the attention of the Securities and Exchange Commission (SEC), a federal organization that regulates the investments industry. By 1979 the SEC cited Keating and other key figures at American Financial for failing to fully disclose a number of loan transactions with their employer. As a result of the SEC investigation, Keating and Lindner signed SEC consents agreeing not to violate federal fraud statutes. But they admitted no wrongdoing in the matter of the company's lending practices.

Pulling Profits Out of His Hat

Keating left American Financial in 1976 and headed to Phoenix, Arizona. There Lindner had helped him take control of American Continental Corporation, a home building organization tied to Lindner's Cincinnati operations. Again, Keating entered into questionable deals designed to inflate the company's profits. *Forbes* reported, "American Continental is ostensibly [outwardly] a savings and loan holding company, but in reality it is a financial speculation company with plays in leveraged buyouts, land development, junk bonds, currency trading and heaven knows what else. In past years, this unconventional setup let Keating pull gains out of his hat and show profits."

In February 1984 American Continental purchased Lincoln Savings and Loan, based in Irvine, California. The purchase price of $51 million was three times the value of S&L's stock and twice its net worth. The sale was brokered by **Michael Milken** (see entry in volume 4). As part of the purchase agreement, Keating promised the Federal Home Loan Bank Board that Lincoln would keep its top executives and remain active in home lending. But he kept neither promise. Keating replaced Lincoln's top executives and, although Lincoln traditionally lent money to individuals purchasing homes, the institution's home loans dwindled to just 2 percent of its business.

Instead of making home loans, Keating sank Lincoln's money into land development, junk bonds, stocks, and real estate projects. Many of the investments were poorly handled. For example, land loans were sometimes granted without first appraising the property. By their very nature, junk bonds are speculative and risky. *Forbes* reported that Keating "invested Lincoln's deposits in junk bonds, many of them [later] trading at prices far below what he initially paid." Some of Lincoln's real estate projects also failed to deliver a profit.

In one such case, Lincoln poured more than $275 million into the plush Phoenician resort in Scottsdale, Arizona. As explained in *Forbes* magazine this, too, was a risky venture:

> American Continental officials say they'll break even with a nightly room rate of $225 and 70 percent occupancy [i.e., 70 percent of the resort's rooms, on average, would have to be occupied by guests]. Greg Nilan, a lodging expert with Pannell Kerr Forster in Phoenix, thinks the break-even rate has to be $350 to $400 a night [per room] at 65 percent occupancy. Scottsdale is overbuilt with luxury hotels. Two other hotels, with

The Securities and Exchange Commission

An agency of the United States government, the Securities and Exchange Commission (SEC), was created by the Securities Exchange Act of 1934 and is responsible for protecting the interests of the public and investors in connection with the public sale of corporate securities. The SEC's five members are appointed by the U.S. president and confirmed by the Senate for terms of five years.

a total of nearly 1,000 rooms, have opened there in the last two years. Another 600-room luxury hotel opened in nearby Tempe. Top rate in the area last year: $200. [In other words, to break even, the Phoenician would have to charge higher prices than any other luxury lodgings in the region.]

CREATIVE ACCOUNTING

Keating also used a deceptive tax-sharing plan to funnel money from the Lincoln S&L into its parent company, American Continental. Between 1986 and 1988, $94.8 million was transferred from Lincoln to American Continental. Meanwhile, Keating and his relatives enjoyed salaries, stock awards, and bonuses totaling about $34 million.

By March 1986 a routine federal audit of Lincoln revealed that the S&L had broken a rule limiting how much a savings and loan institution could directly invest. The rule was set to limit investments to 10 percent of a company's total assets, but Lincoln exceeded that amount by $600 million. In a report to the Federal Home Loan Bank Board, the accounting firm Kenneth Leventhal wrote (as quoted in *Forbes*), "Seldom in our experience as accountants have we experienced a more egregious [glaring] example of the misapplication of general accepting accounting principals." Further, Leventhal suggested that more than half of the earnings Lincoln posted over the course of five years had been falsely reported.

CHARLES KEATING, SOVEREIGN NATION

The auditors recommended that officials in Washington D.C. take steps to restrict Lincoln's questionable lending and accounting procedures. By November 1986 five U.S. senators had rallied to Keating's defense. The so-called Keating Five—Senators John McCain and Dennis DeConcini of Arizona, Alan Cranston of California, Donald Riegle of Michigan, and John Glen of Ohio—had received a total of nearly $1.4 million in campaign contributions from Keating. In fact, Keating's political contributions did not end there; he had also donated money to twenty-four members of Congress.

On April 2, 1987, Edwin Gray, then chairman of the Federal Home Loan Bank Board, attended a meeting with all the senators except Riegle. "The group gathered in DeConcini's office at the senator's invitation," reported *Washington Monthly*. "During the meeting, DeConcini held on his lap a memorandum that outlined Keating's terms and conditions, as though Keating were a sovereign [all-powerful] nation. If Gray would call off his dogs and stop writing new rules, DeConcini explained, Keating would agree to make some home loans. Gray, though shaken by this exhibition of Keating's raw political power, refused."

Gray told *Newsweek* magazine that: the senators "came to me like lawyers arguing for a client…. This is a story of incredible corruption. I can't call it anything else." Recognizing Gray as a threat, Keating began pushing to have the chairman removed

Charles Keating lost millions of dollars in the Lincoln Savings & Loan scandal and testified about the amount of involvement of five U.S. senators. *Reproduced by permission of AP/Wide World Photos.*

from the Federal Home Loan Bank Board. If that failed, it was reported that he was prepared to attempt to hire Gray himself.

LICENSED TO DEFRAUD

But Chairman Gray remained steadfast in pursuing the case against Keating. In May 1987 examiners recommended that the federal government seize Lincoln for operating in an unsound manner and mishandling its assets. "With the question of a federal takeover of Lincoln Savings and Loan hanging fire," *Newsweek* wrote, "the bank board underwent a sudden revolution. Gray...was replaced as chairman by M. Danny Wall... [who] rejected a recommendation from his own enforcement supervisor that Lincoln be taken over by the government." Keating found an ally in Wall, the new chairman of the board.

Chairman Wall's dealings with Keating were unconventional, at best. He allowed Keating to attempt to change his primary regulator, in the hopes of finding a more sympathetic one. (A bank's primary regulator is a committee or company that is in charge of enforcing banking rules and regulations.) Although that attempt failed, Keating was able to negotiate a memorandum of understanding (a plan outlining an agreement and/or compromise) with the Federal Home Loan Bank Board. As reported in the *Washington Monthly,* William Black, the attorney for the San Francisco regulators pursuing Keating and the former deputy director of the Bank Board, told the Banking Committee of the U.S. House of Representatives that Keating's "memorandum of understanding [MOU]" was "the worst so-called enforcement document in history.... The Agreement and the MOU were a virtual cease and desist order...against the Bank Board."

CHARGED WITH CHEATING "THE WEAK, MEEK, AND IGNORANT"

Eventually, no matter how strong his political ties, Keating was forced to admit defeat. On April 12, 1989, American Continental filed for bankruptcy protection. Lincoln was seized by the government, leaving about twenty-thousand investors holding worthless junk bonds. Many of Keating's victims were retired and elderly. *Newsweek* later reported that "in a California lawsuit

"Success," but at a Price

"It is almost impossible to find anyone who likes Charles Keating."
—*Fortune* magazine

Federal Deregulation

During the 1980s Congress passed a series of laws, including the Garn-St. Germain Act, that deregulated (removed government controls from) the U.S. thrift industry, which is made up of savings and loan associations, savings banks, and credit unions. Before the deregulation of that industry, savings and loan associations performed only the following functions: they received savings deposits of individuals, invested them, and provided a modest return to depositors in the form of interest.

The federal deregulation of the 1980s gave savings banks a great deal more freedom. Such institutions were now allowed to convert themselves into capital stock corporations and had access to new lending powers. Deregulation also allowed the ceilings (maximums) on interest rates to be removed and made it easier for large banks to take over smaller, struggling banks.

Some bankers abused these new freedoms, resulting in enormous losses of customer deposits, which are protected by the federal government (and therefore funded by all taxpayers). The case of Charles Keating is a clear-cut example of such abuses. After deliberately selling worthless stock to thousands of investors, he drove Lincoln Savings & Loan to ruin. The government bailout of that institution, which was somewhere from $2.5 million to $2.5 billion, was the most expensive bailout to date. The Keating scandal prompted the government to tighten regulations of savings institutions.

against Lincoln, a witness has produced an internal [Lincoln] memo to its bond salesmen, telling them: 'Always remember the weak, meek and ignorant are always good targets.'"

The federal government and the state of California filed about ninety charges against Keating, his family members, and associates. The charges included conspiracy, racketeering, and fraud. Keating and others were also accused of defrauding Lincoln and falsifying profits by reversing $82 million in real estate deals.

CHARGED AND RECHARGED

In 1991 the state of California convicted Keating on seventeen counts of securities fraud, for which he was sentenced to ten years in prison. Two years later, he received a twelve-and-a-half year sentence in federal court after being found guilty of seventy-three of the charges against him. Keating was released in October 1996, after serving less than five years, when both convictions were overturned. Rulings determined that the state's charges were invalid, while the federal case was thought to have been prejudiced by jurors' knowledge of the state conviction.

On January 15, 1998, the federal court restored the earlier convictions against Keating. But once again, the state's conviction was put aside—this time because the judge had improperly instructed the jury. In April 1999, Keating made a deal with prosecutors, pleading guilty to four counts of fraud and was released from prison. He served only four and a half years in prison but faces several civil judgments against him that could leave him close to bankruptcy for the remainder of his life. The government's bailout of Lincoln is estimated to cost tax payers of somewhere between $2.5 million and $2.5 billion—a sum that will probably take decades to pay off.

For More Information

Chancellor, Edward. *Devil Take the Hindmost: A History of Financial Speculation.* New York: Farrar, Straus and Giroux, 1999, p. 276.

Charles Keating and the S&L crisis. http://ronbell.tripod.com/keating.htm (accessed on August 2, 2002).

Davis, L. J. "Will Charlie Keating Ride Again? Congress Is Once Again Looking at Banking Deregulation. Will It Ignore the Lessons of the Past?" *Washington Monthly* (March 1997).

Giltenan, Edward. "Gall in the Family." *Forbes* (July 8, 1991).

Glassman, James K. "The Great Banks Robbery: Deconstructing the S&L Crisis." *The New Republic* (October 8, 1990).

Kohn, George Childs. *The New Encyclopedia of American Scandal.* New York: Checkmark Books, 2001, p. 217.

Labich, Kenneth, et al. "The Year's 25 Most Fascinating Business People." *Fortune* (January 1, 1990).

Lavin, Cheryl. "Charlie's Web: The Tangled Financial Network That Keating Built." *Chicago Tribune* (January 14, 1990).

O'Shea, James. *The Daisy Chain: How Borrowed Billions Sank a Texas S&L.* New York: Pocket Books, 1991, pp. 39, 205, 207.

Rudnitsky, Howard. "Good Timing, Charlie." *Forbes* (November 27, 1989).

Sifakis, Carl. *The Encyclopedia of American Crime.* 2d ed. New York: Facts on File, 2001, vol. 2: p. 480.

Sloan, Allan, and John H. Taylor. "Mr. Keating, Meet Mr. Short." *Forbes* (December 26, 1988).

Taylor, John H. "Trust Me." *Forbes* (October 17, 1988).

Sante Kimes

1935

AKA: First names: Sandra, Sandy, Santee, Santa. Last names: Guerin, Jacobson, Powers, Saligman, Singer, Singhrs, Walker.

Kenneth Kimes

1975

AKA: Manny Guerin

Swindlers, Robbers, Murderers

"They are the most evil, ingenious con artists we've seen in a long time."

--A senior law enforcement official, quoted in the *New York Times*

During the 1990s Sante and Kenneth Kimes, a mother-and-son crime team, crisscrossed the country working scams including insurance fraud, check fraud, and theft. They were caught with a stolen car in 1998, in which police found detailed records of crimes and personal items belonging to Irene Silverman, a socialite who had disappeared from New York City. Without a body or physical evidence, the Kimeses were found guilty of 118 charges in 2001, including Silverman's murder, which was apparently carried out as part of a plot to defraud her of her $7-million townhouse. They have also been charged or implicated in two other murders.

WILL THE REAL SANTE KIMES PLEASE STAND UP?

Considered to be one of the most notorious con artists of our time, Sante Kimes led a life veiled in secrecy. Even the facts about her childhood are distorted by exaggeration and outright lies. In his memoir *Son of Grifter,* Sante's first son, Kent Walker, describes the story she told while she was on trial for enslavement in 1985. The tale was an attempt to gain sympathy from the jurors.

The Sante Kimes who was on trial claimed that she was born in Oklahoma City [Oklahoma] on July 24, 1934, to a thirty-four-year-old mother of Dutch extraction, Mary Van Horn, and a forty-four-year-old farm laborer father with a background thought exotic in those days. Prame Singhrs was an East Indian. Sante Kimes was born Sante Singhrs, an Okie [Oklahoman] with a twist. She said she had an older brother, Kareem, and an older sister, Reba. Before the slavery trial, I'd never heard Mom so much as mention siblings.

The story went on. After her family left Oklahoma for Los Angeles, California, Sante claimed that her father abandoned his wife and children. Struggling to support her family, Sante's

Sante and Kenneth Kimes were found guilty of second degree murder and 117 other charges, ranging from conspiracy to robbery.
Reproduced by permission of AP/Wide World Photos.

mother turned to prostitution. Soon, her daughter followed. Or so she said. Kent Walker continues:

> By the time she was eight, Sante was allegedly a street kid in Studio City [California], just over the hill from Hollywood in the San Fernando Valley. According to what she told a court appointed shrink [psychiatrist], she scrounged food for herself and her siblings while my alcoholic grandma turned tricks [practiced prostitution].

As her story goes, Sante claimed she was later adopted by Edwin and Mary Chambers, thanks to the intervention of a woman named Dottie Selligman. Sante's name was then changed to Sandra Chambers. Sante also told the court-appointed psychiatrist that she had been abused by men while she was living on the streets of Studio City and that her adoptive father, Edwin Chambers, had raped her repeatedly. Kent Walker questioned his mother's accusation against Chambers: "I seriously doubt the stuff about Grandpa Chambers raping her," he wrote. "Mom leveled those charges in 1985. Not only was the man dead, but sex-abuse claims had become a newly popular means of seeking mercy from the court."

While it is difficult to separate facts from fiction about Sante's early life, one thing is clear—she was known as a liar and a thief even as a school girl.

EASY TO LOVE, EASY TO HATE

In 1957 Sante married Ed Walker, a contractor from Carson City, Nevada. The couple's only son, Kent Walker, learned from his mother how to shoplift and steal cars. Walker wrote in his memoir that at one time Sante punched him in the face to avoid being arrested for shoplifting. When the police arrived, the shopkeeper—whom Sante accused of punching her son—was arrested instead. Sante went free, while her son went to the hospital for stitches. Nevertheless, Walker felt a strong attachment to his mother, who could be both loving and unpredictable. "There was absolutely no one who was easier to love than Sante Kimes," he said. "And no one was easier to hate. She was a walking contradiction."

In 1967 Sante and Ed Walker split. The following year they were divorced. Sante's mission, she told her son, was to marry a millionaire. Kenneth Kimes Sr. fit the bill perfectly. A self-made multimillionaire, Kimes owned a construction company that built motels in California, including a prime property across the street from Disneyland. Sixteen years older than Sante, the shy and quiet builder fell madly in love with the flamboyant younger woman and the two were married in 1970. "It seems remarkable that someone who'd amassed a fortune of twenty million dollars as a legitimate businessman would fall for my mother and stay with her," Kent Walker wrote about his mother's relationship with Kimes. "People well acquainted with my stoic, low-key, and very formal stepfather and my excessive, glad-handing mother couldn't figure out the attraction."

But Kent knew what part of the attraction was:

> From their earliest days together, when he hired a detective to spy on her, Ken [Kimes] knew where Mom got her cars, furniture, fur coats, and knick-knacks. Not only did he not mind, he approved of her larceny [theft]. He drove cars he knew were hot [stolen], and laughed about it. And admired Mom.... He enjoyed the battle.

LITTLE LORD KENNY

In 1975 Sante and Ken Kimes had a son, Kenneth "Kenny" Kimes Jr. Sante believed that because he was the son of a millionaire, Kenny deserved a life of privilege and special treatment. By the time he was four, she hired tutors who worked with him eight hours a day. Public school was out of the question. She picked out her son's clothing and chose his friends. In 1998 a neighbor of the Kimes explained to a *Time* magazine reporter, "She told me her son was a genius, and mine wasn't, so she didn't want them together." A hyperactive child who was slow to talk, Kenny led an isolated existence marked by the domineering presence of his mother.

In August 1985 Sante and Ken Kimes Sr. were arrested on federal charges of enslavement. After smuggling young Mexican women into the United States, the Kimeses had them work as maids in their home. But they did not pay them or give them time off, and the women had no way out of their situation. Ken Kimes, who admitted to knowing about the slavery and doing nothing to prevent it, was given a suspended sentence and fined $70,000. Sante was sentenced to five years in prison.

THE GOLDEN YEARS

Young Kenny's life changed almost over night. Just eleven years old when his mother went to prison, he grew closer to his father, who showered him with affection. Kimes allowed his son to attend school and to have friends of his own. Kenny was enjoying his "golden years," his friend, Vittorio Raho, later recalled, "His father was a very kind guy, a good friend." Kimes bought his son a piano, made sure a pool was installed in the back yard before his birthday, and treated his son's friends like family. Once he took Kenny, Vittorio, and another friend to a hotel on Los Angeles's fashionable Rodeo Drive, where they ate breakfast in bed and later went shopping.

Kenny's golden years came to an abrupt end in 1989 when his mother, who had served only three years of her sentence, was released from prison. Kenny had refused even to speak to his mother on the phone during her imprisonment. When Sante returned, she regained control of her son's life. She had him transferred to a new school and the family moved to another home. Friends were left behind. Eventually Kenny withdrew from school, again to be tutored at home.

When Ken Kimes Sr. died in 1994, he left behind a son who was quickly becoming an angry young man. Kenny once attacked and beat his mother. In college in November 1995, a female student filed a restraining order against him. But eventually the hostile young man, who claimed to hate his mother, became his mother's partner in crime. Together they went on a crime spree that included arson, car theft, insurance fraud—and even murder.

ONE BAD CHECK AND A MISSING BALLERINA

In 1998 Sante and Ken Kimes moved into a lavish apartment in a mansion on New York's East Side. Their landlord was Irene Silverman, an eccentric former ballerina. After the death of her husband, a wealthy investor, Silverman had divided her

Not a Loving Son

"He hated her. He hated her. It's unbelievable that she could make him do these crimes." --A former neighbor in Las Vegas, referring to Kenny and Sante Kimes, quoted in the *New York Times*

Despite frequent arguments, Ken Kimes Jr. never left the side of his domineering mother and followed in her con artist ways. *Reproduced by permission of Getty Images.*

$7-million Fifth Avenue townhouse into apartments, which she rented to a well-screened and well-heeled clientele. Located near Central Park, the apartments were leased for more than $6,000 a month. Using a false identity, Ken Kimes had approached Silverman about renting one of her apartments. During their conversation, he happened to drop the name of one of her friends. Although typically cautious, the elderly

Terms of Endearment

The actor Mary Tyler Moore, who has appeared in various popular television series and movies, portrayed Sante Kimes in the CBS movie *Like Mother, Like Son: The Strange Story of Sante and Kenny Kimes,* which aired in 2001. To get into character, Moore spent hours with a psychiatrist so that she could better understand the behavior of sociopaths (individuals who have no sense of moral responsibility or social consciousness). She also visited Riker's Island, the New York prison where Sante and Kenny Kimes were held during their three-month trial.

Moore explained her interpretation of Sante Kimes to a *Boston Herald* reporter:

I'm not trying to exonerate [clear] her for anything she did. I'm just trying to play her with some empathy for the experiences that she had in life. If you were to speak to her today, she does not believe she did anything wrong, and that's what fascinated me about this type of mental disorder.

She was paranoid. She thought the whole world was against her. Now there were people out there who were out to get her, certainly with good reason. And she would strike out first. It was a form of self defense.... She was a sick person, very sick, but I would not call her evil, inappropriate and warped.

woman allowed Kimes to con his way into her home. It would prove to be a fatal mistake.

On July 5, 1998, the eighty-two-year-old Silverman disappeared. That same day Sante and Ken Kimes were arrested for passing a bad check. Before arriving in New York, the Kimeses had purchased a 1997 green Lincoln Town Car in California. Their check, made out for $14,972, bounced (was unpaid by the bank, due to insufficient funds) and the car dealer filed a complaint. That complaint led law enforcement officials to the Kimeses in New York where they were arrested and soon linked with Silverman's disappearance.

Inside the Kimeses' Town Car was proof that they had schemed to con Silverman out of millions of dollars. Police found blank power-of-attorney forms and rent receipts bearing the elderly woman's signature. They also found a computer, a loaded pistol, and blood. But the blood did not belong to Silverman.

The Kimeses claimed to know nothing about the disappearance of Irene Silverman. No body was found and no physical evidence proved that they were involved in her disappearance. But the circumstantial evidence (evidence or conclusions drawn from the situation) was overwhelming. On May 18, 2000, after a three-month trial, Sante and Ken Kimes were found guilty of second-degree murder—and 117 other charges, ranging from conspiracy to robbery, eavesdropping, and illegal weapons possession. Each was sentenced to more than one hundred years in prison.

For More Information

"California Dreamin'." *People* (December 4, 2000).

"End of the Line." *People* (June 5, 2000).

Guthrie, Marisa. "Not-So-Ordinary People: Mary Tyler Moore Takes on the Mother of All Roles." *Boston Herald* (May 20, 2001).

Havill, Adrian. "Mother and Son Murder Team: Sante and Kenny Kimes." *The Crime Library.* http://www.crimelibrary.com/classics6/kimes/ (accessed on August 2, 2002).

"He Said 'No.'" *People* (May 7, 2001).

"The Lady Vanishes." *People* (July 27, 1998).

McFadden, Robert, and Frank Bruni. "A Twisted Tale of Deceit, Fraud and Violence." *New York Times,* New York Late Edition (July 14, 1998).

Moore, Solomon. "Crime: Information from witnesses links Sante and Kenneth Kimes to killing of Granada Hills resident. Pair are also suspects in New York case." *Los Angeles Times* (October 17, 1998).

Rivera, Elaine. "Trial of the Grifters." *Time* (August 10, 1998).

Vitucci, Clair. "Investigation: Wigs, guns are found in car of Kenneth Kimes and his mother, Sante. Pair are suspected in death of area man." *Los Angeles Times* (July 11, 1998).

Walker, Kent, with Mark Schone. *Son of a Grifter, A Memoir by the Other Son: The Twisted Tale of Sante and Kenny Kimes, The Most Notorious Con Artists in America.* New York: William Morrow, 2001.

Katya Komisaruk

(Susan Alexis Komisaruk)

1958
Trespasser

Katya Komisaruk is a firm believer in public protest as a way to bring about government and social reforms. Before she became a lawyer, she committed a total of thirty-one acts of civil disobedience—nonviolent but illegal acts to call attention to issues ranging from homelessness to the U.S. military's involvement in Central America. Her last act of civil disobedience was a protest against nuclear arms. On June 2, 1987 she broke into Vandenberg Air Force Base in California and destroyed a government computer. After doing so, she left behind cookies, flowers, and a poem. She was later arrested by police and charged with sabotage and destruction of government property. **(See original entry on Komisaruk in *Outlaws, Mobsters, & Crooks,* Volume 2.)**

ON THE OTHER SIDE OF THE LAW

Sentenced to five years in prison for the Vandenberg incident, Komisaruk served only two years at the federal penitentiary in Spokane, Washington and was released on parole for the remainder of her sentence. While in jail she studied law with a fellow inmate and helped other inmates file lawsuits. For that, she claims, she was forced by prison authorities to clean toilets rather than work in the library.

Prior to her release in 1990, Komisaruk applied to several law schools. Accepted at prestigious universities, including Stanford, Cornell, and the University of California at Berkeley, she chose to attend law school at Harvard University in Cambridge, Massachusetts. While still on parole, she completed law school and in 1993 was admitted to the California bar (legal system)—in spite of her arrest record. To get around the American Bar Association's rule against allowing convicted criminals to practice law, she successfully claimed that the crimes she committed did not represent moral failings.

Unlike many of her peers, Komisaruk had no interest in working for a law firm or large corporation. She studied law for the same reasons she vandalized Vandenberg Air Force Base—to fight what she believes to be injustice. "Lawyers," she explained to the *Los Angeles Times*, "should be advocates for justice and for social change."

"When I think of Katya, I feel at least some of my work has been really worthwhile," Komisaruk's former defense attorney, Leonard Weinglass told the *Los Angeles Times*. "To have a client go from being arrested, convicted, imprisoned and then to law school and now be a lawyer for the poor and disenfranchised [unprivileged], it makes me feel life is worthwhile."

CIVILLY DISOBEDIENT

Komisaruk's legal clients protest a wide variety of issues, from misbehavior by oil companies to the death penalty and the development of biogenetically engineered foods. Besides defending clients, she also trains political activist groups in the fine art of civil disobedience. She speaks from experience to offer helpful tactics. Her advice includes: stick together (as a group) and never cooperate with authorities; never touch a police officer, which could bring charges of battery or resisting arrest; and try to create such a nuisance that judge and prosecu-

A Political Closing

At her trial, Komisaruk was not allowed to mount a political defense. But in her closing argument she managed to make her political point against nuclear weapons of mass destruction clear. "You must decide whether an instrument of mass destruction can ethically be considered property." — Komisaruk to the jurors at her trial in 1988, quoted in the *Los Angeles Times*

Katya Komisaruk often took part in World Trade Organization (WTO) protests and helped legally advise protestors who were arrested. *Reproduced by permission of Corbis Corporation.*

tors simply give up on the case. Komisaruk has also taken her passion and knowledge into the academic environment, teaching a course on the history of civil disobedience at the University of California at Los Angeles (UCLA) school of law.

Although Oakland, California, is her home, Komisaruk travels around the country to counsel and defend activists. She advised World Trade Organization (WTO) conference protesters during their anti-globalization demonstrations that began in Seattle in November 1999. As protesters were subjected to tear gas, she attempted to negotiate a settlement with police. She stood in the rain for fifteen hours, shouting legal advice to arrested protesters who were being held on a bus. She also held up large signs so that the demonstrators could read her legal advice. When Komisaruk's clients went to trial, she succeeded in having charges against 280 protesters dropped because of insufficient evidence that they had blocked traffic or failed to disperse as charged during the WTO meetings.

Komisaruk leads a loosely organized group called the Midnight Special Legal Collective, which grew out of the WTO protests. Much of her income comes from donations to that group. After the WTO demonstration, she was involved in protests against Republican policies, staged during the Republican National Convention in Philadelphia in 2000 and she played a key role in demonstrations at the Democratic National Convention in Los Angeles the same year.

For More Information

Bevilacqua, Simon. "A Case of Blind Justice." *Sunday Tasmanian (Hobart, Australia)* (December 30, 2001): p. 007.

Robin, Joshua. "Bringing 1st Amendment Fight to WTO Trials Attorney Specializes in Civil Disobedience." *Seattle Times* (January 7, 2000): p. B-1.

Weinstein, Henry, and Ted Rohrlich. "Katya Komisaruk, who trains and defends protesters, has been there—and done that." *Los Angeles Times* (August 17, 2000): p. E-1.

Nicholas Leeson

February 25, 1967
Swindler

Nicholas "Nick" Leeson was twenty-eight when he bankrupted England's Barings Bank, one of the world's oldest lending institutions. He was working for the bank's Singapore office when he got into trouble in late 1994. His previously successful trading strategy was thrown off by changes in the Singapore International Monetary Exchange (SIMEX) market, specifically Japan's Nikkei index. By February 1995 he and his wife had fled the country. After he was apprehended in Germany, Leeson was returned to Singapore, where he served a sentence for forgery and was released in 1999. He wrote the book *Rogue Trader,* which was made into a movie starring Ewan McGregor.

ON THE WAY TO BARINGS BANK

Born in Watford, a suburb of London, England, Leeson grew up in a working-class environment. His father, Harry, worked as a plasterer and the family lived in a government-funded housing project. Private school was out of the question.

Although not a brilliant student, Leeson applied himself and was chosen to attend Parmiter's grammar school, an institution for bright boys whose families cannot afford to pay for tuition at one of Britain's elite schools. But after failing his final math exams, he did not go on to attend a university.

At eighteen, Leeson took a job as a junior clerk at Coutts & Company, a private bank. In 1987 he moved to the investment banking firm of Morgan Stanley, where he continued to work as a clerk. Two years later he joined London's Barings Bank—a stunning accomplishment for a young man with no college education.

Founded in 1762, the Barings Bank was considered a landmark British institution. Governed for two centuries by descendants of Francis Baring, the bank helped finance the Napoleonic wars (1800–15), the Louisiana Purchase (a treaty the United States signed with France in 1803), and the construction of the Canadian Pacific Railway. Although primarily an investment establishment, the bank had a number of wealthy individual clients, including Britain's Queen Elizabeth II (1926–).

Throughout most of its life, Barings was a conservative institution. But at the time that Leeson joined the bank, it was undergoing radical cultural changes. Senior, conservative staff members soon found themselves working with young, hotshot traders who favored short-term, high-risk gains over safer long-term investment strategies. Leeson was a young hotshot.

The Truth about Derivatives

Nicholas Leeson made—and lost—a fortune by trading in derivatives, highly complex financial products that can either reduce or intensify risk. *Time* magazine offered a helpful description of derivatives:

Derivatives, which are based on such real assets as stocks and bonds, work like most professional betting games…always producing a winner and a loser. The bettors put up their money, and the people who run the casino—a bank, a brokerage house, or an insurance company—figure out ways to pass on the risks. Companies use derivatives to hedge against changes in interest rates, foreign-exchange rates, and commodities prices. Mutual funds and pension funds use them to protect their stock and bond investments. Major banks, brokerage firms, and insurance companies write them for customers.

Some blame derivatives trading in general for the collapse of the Barings Bank. Most, however, attribute the catastrophe to human error—to the actions of a reckless rogue trader or the failure of management to govern the bank's activities, or both. Experts caution the banking industry not to condemn derivative financial instruments on the basis of isolated instances of abuse.

WORKING BOTH SIDES OF THE FENCE

In 1992 Leeson was transferred to Singapore, where Barings was slowly expanding its small trading operation. That same year, he met and married Lisa Sims, a young Barings clerk from Kent, England. At first, Leeson continued to work in the "back office," settling accounts. But Barings Singapore was short-staffed and Leeson knew the market. Soon, he was working both sides—conducting transactions in the "front office" as a member of Barings's trading team and settling accounts in the back office.

In his 1996 autobiography *Rogue Trader,* Leeson described the intoxicating feeling of moving to the front office.

> When I first stepped out on to the trading floor, I could smell and see the money. Throughout my time at Barings I had been inching closer and closer to it, and in Singapore I was suddenly there. I'd been working in various back offices for almost six years, pushing paper money around, sorting out other people's problems. Now, out on the trading floor, I could work with instant money—it was hanging in the air right in front of me, invisible but highly charged, just waiting to be earthed. As I watched the traders all screaming at each other in their red jackets, I imagined an electrical thunderstorm. There was lightning in the air, and all I had to do was give the right signals and it would charge through me as if I were a copper conductor.

Since he was also working in the back office, Leeson was allowed to settle his own accounts. It was a highly unusual arrangement. In direct contrast to the bank's normal practices, no reporting procedures monitored what Leeson was doing in Singapore. In his autobiography he described that his "reporting lines were as hazy and inbred as the Barings family tree itself.... It was a bizarre structure, and one which allowed me to run my own show without anyone interfering."

In March 1992 James Bax, the regional manager for Barings South Asia, sent a memo to the London office that would later prove to be prophetic.

> My concern is that once again we are in danger of setting up a structure which will subsequently prove disastrous and with which we will succeed in losing

In His Own Words

"I had been surprisingly unmoved by how the numbers had added up--for me it was the principle which mattered." --Nick Leeson, in *Rogue Trader*

either a lot of money or client goodwill or probably both.... In my view it is critical that we should keep clear reporting lines, if this office is involved in SIMEX at all.

Much to their later regret, Leeson's superiors did not heed Bax's warning.

ERROR ACCOUNT 88888

Leeson began to trade in simple derivatives, which are complex and risky financial products. Wildly successful trading on the SIMEX, he contributed substantially to the bank's earnings. In the first half of 1994, Barings's total profits stood at $87 million; of that amount, the Singapore office had brought in $30 million.

Leeson was rewarded for his efforts. He received an annual salary estimated to be as high as $350,000 and he boasted that he was promised a $2-million bonus. He lived in a $9,000-a-month condominium (paid for by Barings) in a fashionable neighborhood of Singapore. He drove an expensive car and cultivated a taste for fine wine.

Bank authorities noted the dangerous potential of Leeson's dual role in Singapore. In August 1994 a Barings internal audit (quoted in *Rogue Trader*) reported:

> The audit found that while the individual controls over BFS's systems and operations are satisfactory, there is significant risk that the controls could be overridden by the General Manager [Nick Leeson]. He is the key manager in the front and back office and can thus initiate transactions on the Group's behalf and then ensure that they are settled and recorded according to his own instructions....
>
> This represents an excessive concentration of powers; companies commonly divide responsibility for initiating, settling and recording transactions among different areas to reduce the possibility of error and fraud....
>
> In normal circumstances it would not be desirable for one individual to combine the role of dealing and trading manager with those of settlements and

accounting manager. Given the lack of experienced and senior staff in the back office, we recognize that the General Manager must continue to take an active role in the detailed operations of both the front and the back office.

The audit concluded that while Nick Leeson represented a serious risk to the Barings, his departure would seriously hurt the bank's profitability. But the audit had overlooked something in Leeson's records: The trader had created a secret account—titled error account 88888—to hide the enormous losses he had begun to sustain. That error account would prove to be the downfall of Barings.

You bet on red, you lose

Toward the end of 1994 Leeson decided to make what he considered to be a safe bet to make up for more than $80 million in losses. He wagered that Tokyo's Nikkei 225 index (a system rating the top Japanese companies) would not drop below approximately 19,000 points before early March 1995.

On the surface, the plan looked like an easy way to score big profits. The Japanese economy was on the upswing and showed no signs of declining. But on January 7, 1995, a natural disaster proved catastrophic to Leeson's scheme. In Kobe, Japan, an earthquake measuring 7.2 on the Richter scale (a scale, ranging from one to ten, measuring the intensity of an earthquake) devastated the port city and rocked the Japanese financial system. In just one week, the Nikkei index dropped by 7 percent.

Leeson had lost his wager. But he continued to gamble. A Hong Kong trader, quoted in *Newsweek,* later described the strategy Leeson employed: "You bet on red, you lose. You double your bet on red, you lose. But as long as you keep doubling your bet, you will never lose in the end—if you have limitless capital." Leeson, however, did not have limitless capital.

When Leeson requested extra funds for the Singapore operation, Barings obliged, even though Leeson had not disclosed his intent. Bank officials took out an $850,000 loan—a sum greater than the bank's entire capital base—to finance the Singapore branch. At the time, the twenty-seven-year-old Leeson reportedly bragged that he was going to make a fortune and retire by the time he was twenty-eight. That fortune never materialized.

Read the Instructions

"Derivatives are like chainsaws. They are immensely useful, but one should read the instructions first." --Charles Taylor, executive director of an independent financial think-tank called the Group of 30, quoted in *MacLean's*

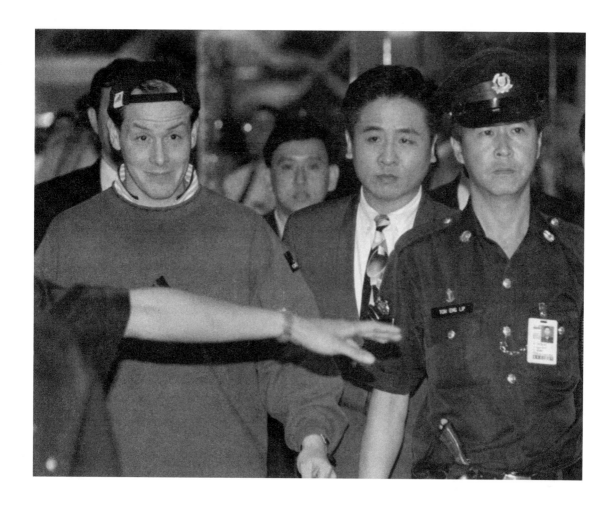

NOT EVEN A SULTAN CAN SAVE A SINKING SHIP

In mid-February 1995, Leeson's colleagues noticed that he seemed to be working even harder than usual. He seemed distracted and he kept going to the men's room to vomit. On Tuesday, February 21, 1995, Leeson put in a full day's work. After leaving the trading floor, he gathered some papers, left a note on his desk, and departed. The note said simply "I'm sorry." He later drove 200 miles (320 kilometers) north of Singapore, to Kuala Lumpur, the capital of Malaysia. He checked into a luxury hotel—using the bank's credit card. The following morning, his wife, Lisa, joined him.

Leeson had left behind $1.4 billion in trading losses—a sum greater than Barings's entire net worth. Finally aware of the cri-

After escaping to Germany and being arrested there, Nick Leeson was transferred to Singapore and turned over to Singapore police to face eleven counts of fraud and forgery.
Reproduced by permission of AP/Wide World Photos.

sis, Barings officials tried desperately to find help. They appealed to the Bank of England and even the Sultan of Brunei, considered the richest man in the world. But Barings was a sinking ship. On February 26, 1995, one of the oldest banks in the world collapsed. The news of the bank's demise came one day after Leeson's twenty-eighth birthday. Later, the Dutch bank ING bought the ruined bank for a token sum of one British pound (worth between one and two dollars).

FROM SEASIDE RESORTS TO A SINGAPORE SLING

Shortly after his hasty departure from Singapore, Leeson reportedly sent a fax to Peter Barings, chairman of the bank. It was a letter of apology, outlining Leeson's activities and losses during his time in Singapore. He wrote that he doubted the two of them would meet again.

Leeson left Kuala Lumpur to meet his wife in Kota Kinabalu, a resort town in Indonesia. There the couple stayed in a luxurious beachfront resort. Next, Leeson purchased two tickets for a Royal Brunei flight to Frankfurt, Germany. He purchased the tickets with cash and used his own name.

Twelve hours after boarding the plane, the Leesons arrived in Frankfurt. German authorities were waiting. Armed with photographs of Nick and Lisa Leeson, they boarded the plane and took the couple into custody. On December 1996, Leeson pled guilty to cheating SIMEX and the accounting firm Coopers & Lybrand. Imprisoned in Changi prison in Singapore, he was released in July 1999. While he was allowed to keep 35 percent of his income from speeches and appearances, the rest was applied to creditors. His book, *Rogue Trader,* was made into a movie by the same name, starring actor Ewan McGregor.

For More Information

"Baring All." *Forbes* (May 6, 1996).

Bellafante, Ginia. "Rogue Trader: Cinemax, June 25." *Time* (June 28, 1999).

Chancellor, Edward. *Devil Take the Hindmost: A History of Financial Speculation.* New York: Farrar, Straus, and Giroux, 1999.

Chua-Eoan, Howard G. "Going for Broke." *Time* (March 13, 1995).

Master of Nothing

"I think he was a dealer who thought he was master of the universe and didn't have the sense to cut his losses." --A London futures trader, quoted in *U.S. News & World Report*

Daglish, Brenda. "Breaking the Bank: The 'Rogue Trader' Who Brought Down Barings Is in Custody but Others Share Blame for the Debacle." *Maclean's* (March 13, 1995).

Kaye, Stephen D. "Ripples from a Fallen Bank." *U.S. News & World Report* (March 13, 1995).

Leeson, Nick, with Edward Whitley. *Rogue Trader: How I Brought Down Barings Bank and Shook the Financial World.* New York: Little, Brown and Company, 1996.

Miller, Annetta. "The Rogue Trader Speaks." *Newsweek* (September 18, 1995).

Mosser, Mike. "The Rogues Among Us." *Futures* (August 2000).

Nusbaum, David, Jack Reerink, and Portia Richardson. "Barings' Apocalypse." *Futures* (April 1995).

Powell, Bill, Daniel Pederson, and Michael Elliot. "Busted!" *Newsweek* (March 13, 1995).

"Rogue Trader." *The Economist (U.S. edition)* (February 24, 1996).

"Rogue Trader to Walk Free." *cnnmoney.* http://money.cnn.com/1999/07/02/worldbiz/leeson/ (accessed on August 2, 2002).

"Trading Places." *Maclean's* (July 12, 1999).

Nathan Leopold

1906
1971

AKA: Babe, Morton D. Ballard

Richard Loeb

1907
1936

AKA: Dickie, Louis Mason

Murderers

Leopold and Loeb killed "not for money, not for spite, not for hate. They killed as they might kill a spider or fly, for the experience."

--Attorney Clarence Darrow, quoted in *Crimes of the Century*

In the 1920s two wealthy, gifted University of Chicago students kidnapped and murdered fourteen-year-old Bobby Franks. They were convinced they could commit the "perfect crime." Their notorious case became the first to be called the "crime of the century."

SONS OF WEALTH AND PRIVILEGE

Leopold and Loeb shared similar backgrounds. Both Chicago natives, they were highly educated, intelligent—and spoiled by wealth and privilege. The son of a successful South Side manufacturer, Nathan "Babe" Leopold received an extravagant allowance from his indulgent parents, who allowed him a great deal of freedom. After his mother, Florence, died, he threw himself into his studies. With an IQ (intelligence quotient) estimated at 200 or above (well above what is considered to be genius), he was a brilliant student. He graduated from the University of Chicago when he was just eighteen years old. At the time he was fluent in nine languages and had become an expert in botany (the study of plants) and ornithology (the study of birds). A shy and bookish young man, Leopold had physical defects including malformed adrenal, pineal, thymus, and thyroid glands.

Like Leopold, Richard "Dickie" Loeb was both brilliant and spoiled. The son of a millionaire vice president of Sears, Roebuck and Company, the young man received a weekly allowance of $250—far more than many top executives earned at that time. When he graduated from the University of Michigan at age seventeen, he became that school's youngest graduate. Like Leopold, he suffered from physical and emotional problems. Although outgoing and athletic, he had suicidal tendencies. He may also have suffered from epilepsy, a disorder of the nervous system.

Both graduates of the prestigious Harvard Preparatory School in Chicago, Leopold and Loeb may have known each other growing up. Sometime around 1920 while both men were enrolled at the University of Chicago, they formed a criminal partnership—documented by a signed contract. Together they committed a number of minor crimes, including vandalism, setting fires, and creating false alarms. But Dickie Loeb had something much more serious in mind.

SUPERMAN WANNABES

Leopold had been fascinated by the notion of a superman since his youth. But his superhero was not found in comic books. An avid reader of Friedrich Nietzche (1844–1900), Leopold was attracted to the German philosopher's concept of an *ubermensch* (German, for "superman")—a superior human being who is not bound by common rules of morality.

Loeb had an idea that appealed to Leopold's interest in a Nietzchean superman. He proposed that they commit a "perfect crime"—a crime that could not be solved. It could have no motive and must be free from passion. In short, the perfect crime would be an act of pure will.

In November 1923 the two began plotting their crime. They planned the abduction to look like a kidnapping for ransom. But money was not their motive. In truth, they had no motive. They planned to abduct and kill their young victim simply for the experience—to prove that, as "superior men," they were capable of carrying out a horrible crime without being caught.

It's Never Easy Collecting Money

In his confession, Leopold admitted that the ransom drop had been the most difficult part of their plan. "We had several dozen different plans, all of which were not so good for one reason or another," he confessed. "Finally we hit upon the plan of having money thrown from a moving train after the train had passed a given landmark."

But the most carefully planned part of Leopold and Loeb's scheme never came to fruition. The body of Bobby Franks was discovered before his parents received the ransom demand.

PLANNING MURDER

The young men planned the murder carefully. Early in 1924 they stole a typewriter from Loeb's former fraternity house at the University of Michigan. The two planned to compose the ransom letter on the typewriter, which they believed could not be traced back to them. They created false identities to open bank accounts under the names of Morton D. Ballard (Leopold) and Louis Mason (Loeb) and to rent a Blue Wyllis-Knight touring car.

The young men bought a rope and chisel, with which they planned to subdue their victim. They also purchased hydrochloric acid, which they would later use to make it difficult for anyone to identify the victim's body. They even rehearsed how the ransom money would be delivered to them by throwing boxes off a Chicago train bound for Michigan City, Indiana. The $10,000 ransom would be deposited in the bank account they had opened under false names. But they had no intention of making good on the ransom exchange. They planned to kill their victim before they contacted his parents.

LUCK OF THE DRAW

The kidnappers gave very little thought to choosing a victim. Quite by chance, they settled on Bobby Franks—the fourteen-year-old son of one of Chicago's wealthiest families and a distant cousin to Loeb. Bobby Franks had not been their first choice—the pair first decided to abduct Armand Deutsch. On the afternoon of May 21, 1924, they waited for Deutsch outside the Harvard Preparatory School. But he never appeared. It turned out that Deutsch was spared because he had been at the dentist's office.

The killers then decided to abduct another boy, John Levison. But they lost sight of him before they were able to approach him. Then Bobby Franks appeared. He fit the killers' profile for their victim. He was a small boy, so he could be easily overcome. His family was wealthy, so a ransom request would not arouse suspicion. And because he knew one of his abductors, he would get into their car without attracting attention.

AN IMPERFECT CRIME

Once inside the car, Franks was hit on the head five times with a chisel. Loeb later claimed that Leopold killed the boy, while Leopold claimed it was Loeb. Just who killed the boy was never proved. Many believe that Leopold drove while Loeb attacked the boy from behind, piercing his skull with the chisel. After seeing the bloody result, Leopold reportedly said, "Oh, God, I didn't know it would be like this!" But others think it most likely that Loeb, who knew Bobby Franks, drove the car and invited him to sit next to him in the front seat.

From Chicago, the killers drove east and south along the Lake Michigan shoreline until they neared Hammond, Indiana, where they pulled off the road. After stripping most of the clothes from the body of Bobby Franks, they drove aimlessly as they waited for nightfall. At one point, they stopped to have hot dogs and root beers.

Under cover of darkness, they drove down a dirt road to a deserted marshland surrounding Wolf Lake. "Having arrived at our destination, we placed the body in [a] robe, carried it to the culvert where it was found," Leopold later confessed. "Here we completed the disrobing [removing clothes], then in an attempt to render identification more difficult, we poured hydrochloric acid over the face and body."

Leopold put on rubber boots, and with Loeb's help, forced Franks's body into a large drain pipe. They took the boy's clothing, which they had wrapped in the robe, to avoid leaving evidence behind. But Bobby Franks's killers had left one of the boy's feet exposed and his body was easily discovered. The killers also left a clue to their identity—Nathan Leopold's eyeglasses dropped out of his pocket near where they had hidden the body. By the end of May, the killers had been taken into custody.

Ransom Notes and Red Herrings

Leopold and Loeb sent a ransom letter to the parents of Bobby Franks, the boy they kidnapped. But the ransom demand was simply a red herring, or false clue, to throw investigators off the right track. No one would suspect two boys from multimillionaire families to commit a kidnapping for a mere $10,000. Both boys received generous allowances from their wealthy parents. In fact, Dickie Loeb alone received about $1,000 each month.

DARROW FOR THE DEFENSE

Evidence against the pair mounted. The typewriter and its keys, which the young men had discarded, were found. Investigators determined that some of Loeb's school papers and the ransom note had been typed on the same machine. Confronted with evidence proving their connection to the crime, Loeb confessed and Leopold followed. Each indicated that the other had conceived the plan for the killing and each blamed the other for the actual killing.

There was no question of their guilt. Virtually guaranteed of being convicted, the young men faced the death penalty. Painfully aware that a "not guilty" verdict was not an option, the Leopold and Loeb families hoped only to spare the lives of their sons. On June 2, the two families retained sixty-seven-year-old Clarence Darrow as defense attorney.

Darrow, who was known nationally as "the Great Defender," knew that the public outrage the crime had incited would most probably earn the two killers spots on death row. He decided not to defend their innocence. Instead, he would use the case to put the death penalty on trial. Darrow laid the groundwork carefully. He had his clients plead guilty with mitigating circumstances, arguing that they men were "mentally diseased" and incapable of judging right from wrong.

The trial, which began on July 21, 1924 and by mutual consent of the prosecution and defense, the trial was not conducted before a jury. Still, the courtroom was overcrowded with people from the media. Chief Justice John Caverly of Illinois' Cook County Criminal Court presided. He was not a judicial "grandstander" and had no long-term political ambitions. Darrow—who was a much more persuasive speaker than the prosecution's state attorney, Robert E. Crowe—asked Justice Caverly to consider the morality of the death penalty:

> Your honor stands between the past and the future.
> You may hang these boys; you may hang them by the
> neck until they are dead. But in doing so you will
> turn your face toward the past.... I am pleading for
> the future; I am pleading for a time when hatred and
> cruelty will not rule the hearts of men, when we can
> learn by reason and judgment and understanding
> and faith that all life is worth saving, and that mercy
> is the highest attribute of man.

On September 10, 1924, the verdict was handed down. Caverly spared the killers from execution—not, he said, because the death penalty was unjust, but because Leopold and Loeb were so young. Having avoided being put to death for their crime, they were sentenced to spend the "remainder of their days on earth" in prison. Justice Caverly gave them each a life term for the murder of Bobby Franks, plus ninety-nine years for kidnapping.

Nathan Leopold, center left, and Richard Loeb, center right, who were quickly arrested and found guilty of murder, thought they would never be caught for what they considered to be the "perfect crime." *Reproduced by permission of AP/Wide World Photos.*

ONE SENTENCE, TWO OUTCOMES

First locked up in separate prisons in Joliet, Illinois, Leopold and Loeb were later moved to the same prison. Loeb, who had been a difficult prisoner, was murdered on January 28, 1936, by

Products of the Experiments of Today?

"We have striven to free our youth, to put upon them little or no responsibility; we have permitted and encouraged the casting off of restraints, a contempt for old codes and morals. We have become supine [passive] before the spirit of experiment and the sneer at not being 'new.' And two of the most gifted and brilliant products of the experiments of today are held by the state's attorney, charged with the most revolting crime of the century."
—*Chicago Herald Examiner* reporter Edwin Balmer, quoted in *Leopold and Loeb: The Crime of the Century*

another inmate. Leopold, on the other hand, became a model prisoner who won the respect of guards and prison officials. He enrolled in correspondence courses in advanced mathematics, physics, and classical languages from the University of Iowa.

Interested in prison reform, he persuaded the faculty at the university to help organize correspondence courses for prisoners and to replace textbooks that had been lost in a fire. He also convinced the prison staff to make it easier for inmates to borrow and read books. During World War II (1939–45), he volunteered for medical tests intended to advance knowledge of the causes and treatment of malaria. Some people regarded Leopold's behavior as a self-serving ploy to gain early release. But others were convinced by it. Impressed by Leopold's apparent rehabilitation, Illinois Governor William Stratton commuted his ninety-nine-year sentence to eighty-five years, which improved the possibility for his ultimate parole (early release).

In 1958 Leopold presented his fifth plea for release. Writer Carl Sandburg—with whom Leopold exchanged letters—and University of Iowa professor Helen Williams spoke on his behalf. Shortly before his release, he announced the formation of the Leopold Foundation to aid disturbed children. The foundation was funded in part with proceeds from his *Life Plus 99 Years,* an autobiography serialized by the *Chicago Daily News* and published in book form in 1958. It featured an introduction by crime novelist Erle Stanley Gardner. While the book did not discuss the murder of Bobby Franks, it gave a detailed account of Leopold's life in prison. Most reviewers praised the book.

On March 13, 1958, after thirty-three years in prison, Leopold was released to the custody of the Church of the Brethren, to which he had been converted while in prison. He worked for $10 per month in the church's medical mission at Castañer, in Puerto Rico's hill country, where he taught mathematics and helped raise funds for the church. He also took correspondence courses from the University of Puerto Rico, earning a master of science degree in June 1961. Three years after his release, he married Trudi Feldman Garcia de Quevado. Leopold died of a heart attack in 1971. In accordance with his wishes, his body was donated to the University of Puerto Rico's School of Medicine.

For More Information

Bardsley, Marilyn. "Leopold & Loeb." *The Crime Library.* http://www.crimelibrary.com/loeb/loeb/loebmain.htm (accessed on August 2, 2002).

Geis, Gilbert, and Leigh B. Bienen. *Crimes of the Century: From Leopold and Loeb to O.J. Simpson.* Boston: Northeastern University Press, 1998, pp.13–47.

Gottesman, Ronald, ed. *Violence in America: An Encyclopedia.* New York: Charles Scribner's Sons, 1999, vol. 2: pp. 285–286; vol. 3: pp. 326–327.

Higdon, Hal. *Leopold and Loeb: The Crime of the Century.* Urbana: University of Illinois Press, 1999.

Jerome, Richard. "Playing for Keeps." *People* (June 14, 1999).

Sifakis, Carl. *The Encyclopedia of American Crime.* 2d ed. New York: Facts on File, 2001, vol. 1: pp. 247–248; vol. 2: pp. 520–521.

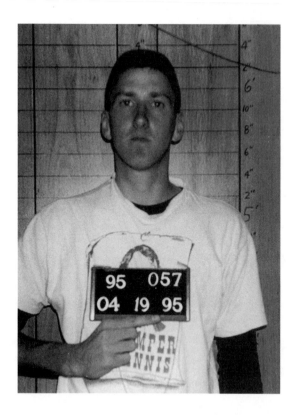

Timothy McVeigh

April 23, 1968
June 11, 2001

Terrorist and Mass Murderer

When a truck bomb exploded in Oklahoma City, Oklahoma, on April 19, 1995, it killed and injured hundreds of innocent victims, including nineteen children under the age of six. The target of the attack was the Murrah Federal Building and its government employees. The nation was stunned to learn that the bombing was not carried out by international terrorists but was the work of an American whose background was similar to that of many other citizens. After being captured in a routine traffic stop, Timothy McVeigh was charged, tried, and sentenced to death for the Oklahoma City bombing. His case divided the American public over the controversial issue of the death penalty. **(See original entry on McVeigh in *Outlaws, Mobsters & Crooks*, Volume 2.)**

FROM SUPERMAX TO TERRE HAUTE

Timothy McVeigh spent most of his sentence in Supermax, a federal penitentiary at the foot of the Rocky Mountains in southern Colorado. He passed his time watching movies on the twelve-inch black-and-white television in his cell, and was allowed to walk in the prison yard ten hours each week. The area where he was held became known as the "bomber's wing" of the prison. In May 1998, "Unabomber" **Ted Kaczynski** (see entry in volume 4) became McVeigh's cell neighbor; also incarcerated in the wing was Ramzi Yousef, who masterminded the February 26, 1993, World Trade Center bombing. But McVeigh's stay in Supermax was brief. In July 1999, he was transferred to the federal death-row facility in Terre Haute, Indiana, where he would await execution.

McVeigh's execution was scheduled for May 16, 2001, but it was postponed until June 11 to allow his defense team to review new evidence. In response to six requests from McVeigh's lawyers, the Federal Bureau of Investigation (FBI) handed over more than four thousand pages of evidence that had not been reviewed at trial. Although the defense team hoped to stall their client's execution, a federal judge in Denver, Colorado (where McVeigh's case had been heard), ruled that the execution date would stand. The decision was backed by the Federal Court of Appeals. McVeigh's team did not appeal to the Supreme Court. Pope John Paul II urged the U.S. government to show mercy for McVeigh and stay the execution. But it was to no avail. The Oklahoma City bomber's execution would go ahead as scheduled.

In His Own Words

"If you have trouble believing that the Justice Department are adept liars—come to one of my pretrial hearings, to the trial itself, or ask Richard Jewell [the original suspect in the Olympic Games bombing in Atlanta, Georgia]. People need to question and analyze what they hear, and ponder the motivations of those spreading the propaganda. The truth lies deeper." —Timothy McVeigh, in a letter published in *Esquire,* May 2001

NATIONWIDE DEBATE

McVeigh's execution added fuel to the national debate over the death penalty. National support for capital punishment (the death penalty) was on the decline, largely due to the number of cases in which death-row inmates were proven innocent by DNA and other forms of evidence that had not been available at their trials. Nevertheless, several public opinion polls showed strong support for McVeigh's execution. Those same polls indicated that Americans have mixed feelings about capital punishment.

Critics of the death penalty question whether it is appropriate to use state-approved killing as a way to reinforce the message that killing is wrong. Elisabeth Semel, director of the American

THE DAILY OKLAHOMAN

McVEIGH GETS DEATH

Tears, Smiles, Words of Anger Greet Verdict

Timothy McVeigh's death sentence was front page news, bringing closure for many of the victims' families and igniting a national debate about capital punishment.
Reproduced by permission of AP/Wide World Photos.

Bar Association's Death Penalty Representation Project, said in the *Los Angeles Daily News* that McVeigh viewed the Oklahoma City bombing as an act of revenge on the U.S. government for the 1993 deaths of the Branch Davidians in Waco, Texas. Semel argued that McVeigh's executioners contributed to an ongoing cycle of revenge. According to *Reason* magazine, her views were shared by many Americans. For some, however, the execution of Timothy McVeigh represented the triumph of good over evil in the nation's worst act of terrorism carried out by an American citizen.

LIVE AND IN COLOR: DEATH BY LETHAL INJECTION

McVeigh's sentence spurred national debate about yet another issue—whether a state-sanctioned execution should be televised for public viewing. Some felt it would help bring clo-

Diary of a Terrorist

The book *American Terrorist: Timothy McVeigh & the Oklahoma City Bombing,* is based on seventy hours of interviews that authors Dan Herbeck and Lou Michel conducted with McVeigh, who was not paid for his contribution and had no editorial control over the final manuscript.

The biography reveals a callous and calculated killer. According to the authors' interviews, McVeigh claimed total responsibility for the Oklahoma City bombing and expressed no remorse over the number of lives lost. He also said he delayed the bombing in order to inflict as much damage as possible and he referred to the children who were killed in the explosion as "collateral damage" in his stand against the federal government.

"We have to say this book was done for historical purposes," Michel told *Newsweek.* "It was the equivalent of sitting down with Lee Harvey Oswald [who killed President John F. Kennedy] or John Wilkes Booth [who assassinated President Abraham Lincoln] and hearing their stories." Co-author Herbeck, too, believes in the historical value of McVeigh's story. "This is arguably the worst crime in the past century in the United States. The book was our job as journalists. If we could turn the clock back and make this event go away, we would. The book was never meant to hurt people in Oklahoma City."

sure to a devastated nation, while others believed that television coverage would only stir up Americans' feelings about the Oklahoma City bombing.

Even McVeigh wanted the execution televised. But the government ruled against it, noting that no state in the nation conducts public executions today. (The last public execution in the United States took place in Owensboro, Kentucky, in 1936.) Even without the ruling, it was reported that network executives had already decided not to televise the convicted killer's death by lethal injection.

Thirty people were allowed to witness McVeigh's execution, while another 250 relatives of the Oklahoma victims watched on closed-circuit television. To prevent any part of the execution from being circulated publicly, video cameras, tape recorders, and cell phones were forbidden.

THE MAIN EVENT

On the day of the execution, the atmosphere outside the Terra Haute facility was circus-like. Crowds of people assem-

"EXECUTED. TIMOTHY MCVEIGH, 33, convicted terrorist whose truck bomb killed 168 people in Oklahoma City on April 19, 1995; by lethal injection; in Terre Haute, Ind. McVeigh spent his last day writing to friends, napping and eating a final meal of mint chocolate-chip ice cream. McVeigh made no final statement, offering instead a handwritten copy of the 1875 poem 'Invictus.' He was the first person executed by the Federal Government in 38 years." —McVeigh's obituary (death notice), published in *Time*, June 25, 2001

bled—some to demonstrate their support or disapproval, others simply to gather. Electronic signs flashed messages directing demonstrators to their respective venues: "Pro demonstrators use Vorhees Park. Anti demonstrators use Fairbanks Park."

Shortly before 7 A.M. on June 11, 2001, McVeigh was strapped onto a gurney. Intravenous lines were inserted to administer the lethal injection. The curtains were opened, allowing witnesses to view the procedure. A ceiling camera, focused on his face, provided closed-circuit viewers with an up-close look of his death. McVeigh stared up at the camera and said nothing. At 7:14 a.m. he was pronounced dead.

POSTSCRIPT

In late 1998 the Oklahoma County grand jury concluded that McVeigh and his accomplice, Terry Nichols, had acted alone. McVeigh, too, had insisted that he had acted on his own. Yet his former trial lawyer, Stephen Jones, later disputed his client's claim. "If McVeigh is saying he acted alone, that is inconsistent with what he told me," he said in the *Daily Oklahoman*. Authorities began to suspect that the Oklahoma bomber had accomplices.

Shattering events such as the Oklahoma City bombing often generate conspiracy theories, many of which bear little or no resemblance to the truth. However, some evidence in the McVeigh trial suggested that the bomber might have acted with the assistance of a foreign power. In 2002 a federal lawsuit was filed against the Republic of Iraq. (A 1996 law permits American victims of terrorism to seek damages from governments identified as terrorist states by the State Department; Iraq was added to the State Department's list of terrorist states in 1990.) The suit accuses Iraq of orchestrating the Oklahoma City attack and seeks $1.5 billion in damages for survivors and relatives of

Field of Dreams

In the area once strewn with the rubble of the Murrah Federal Building, Oklahoma City administrators constructed a $32-million minor-league ballpark dedicated to Oklahoma native Mickey Mantle.

victims. A large portion of that sum constitutes punitive damages—intended to "punish and deter" Iraq from "future actions of this magnitude [size and scope]. Federal agents and prosecutors have said repeatedly that they investigated such claims but found no evidence of a foreign country's involvement."

For More Information

Bayless, Skip. "A Ballpark Rises from the Psychological Rubble." *The (Bergen County, New Jersey) Record* (April 19, 1998): p. S2.

Broadcasting & Cable (April 23, 2001): p. 18.

Buckley, William F., Jr. "On the Right—Watch the Killer Get Killed?" *National Review* (May 28, 2001).

Garvey, Michael O. "Death in Terre Haute: The Execution of Timothy McVeigh." *Commonweal* (July 13, 2001): p. 9.

"Gone, but Not Forgiven; Timothy McVeigh's Execution; the End for McVeigh." *The Economist (U.S. edition)* (June 16, 2001): p. 2.

Hamilton, Arnold. "Iraq Sued in OKC Bombing: Plaintiffs Say Nation Was Behind McVeigh, Seek $1.5 Billion." *Dallas Morning News* (March 16, 2002): p. 31A.

"Milestones." *Time* (June 25, 2001): p. 23.

Morganthau, Tom. "Outcry Over a Killer's Story: in a Controversial New Book, Oklahoma City Bomber Timothy McVeigh's Chilling Lack of Remorse for His Shocking Crime Is Reopening Some Old Wounds as His Date with Death Approaches." *Newsweek* (April 9, 2001): p. 22.

Patterson, John. "Ex-CIA Agent Believes in a John Doe 2." *The Indianapolis Star* (March 23, 2002): p. A12.

"The Prison Letters of Timothy McVeigh." *Esquire* (May 2001): p. 130.

"The Rights and Wrongs; Timothy McVeigh's Execution." *The Economist (U.S. edition)* (May 12, 2001): p. 1.

Tharp, Mike. "No Regrets, No Remorse." *U.S. News & World Report* (April 9, 2001): p. 32.

Wagner, Anne. "Poll Track." *National Journal* (May 19, 2001): p. 1509.

Young, Cathy. "McVeigh to Macbeth." *Reason* (July 2001): p. 20.

Joaquin Murieta

c. 1830
c. 1853 or c. 1878

Bandit and Gunslinger

When considering the life of Joaquin Murieta, it is almost impossible to separate fact from fiction. He became famous for his exploits during the California Gold Rush. Authorities were so determined to catch him that law agents were assigned to kill or capture any man with the first name Joaquin, a common Mexican name. Many people feel Murieta's exploits became exaggerated over time, while others see him as a hero, and others believe he never really existed at all.

MOUNTING TENSIONS NORTH OF THE BORDER

Joaquin Murieta was born in Alamos, in the Mexican state of Sonora, around 1830. His father, who was probably a Maya Indian, worked in the silver mines near Varoyeca, Sonora. His mother is believed to have been descended from Spanish and Moorish ancestors. Documents indicate that before leaving Mexico, the young Murieta attended a Jesuit school in his hometown.

Growing up in Sonora, Murieta was exposed to the violence of warfare. Already unsettled by the Maya and Yaqui Indian revolts of 1825, Sonora was thrown into turmoil when the United States invaded Mexico in 1848. Murieta eventually moved to California, probably to farm and build a better life. But after gold was discovered in the hills of California, he turned to mining. The Foreign Miners' Tax of 1850 imposed a fee on non-Americans, making it difficult for Mexican laborers to support themselves.

Murieta was no exception. Struggling to support a wife, he is believed to have begun trading in wild horses. Meanwhile, tensions continued to mount between white American miners and Mexican workers. According to legend, Murieta's wife, Rosa, was assaulted by white Americans; his brother was hanged; and he was beaten. A series of raids were waged on American mining camps and Murieta was singled out as the ringleader. Some contemporary accounts treat the raids as a response to the wrongs committed against Murieta's family. Other accounts describe the raids as random violence that inflamed anti-Mexican sentiments.

DESPERATELY SEEKING JOAQUIN

By the spring of 1853, Murieta was a wanted man. Blamed for a rash of robberies and assaults in the California countryside, the outlaw "Joaquin" had a substantial reward posted for his capture. Since no one was sure exactly who Joaquin was or what he looked like, it was possible that any law-abiding Mexican could be mistaken for him. For this reason Jose Maria Covarrubias, a member of California's Committee on Military Affairs, urged the state to reconsider the posting. Eventually the reward was dropped. But the hunt for Joaquin was not over.

In May 1853, the California legislature proposed an act allowing a company of mounted rangers to capture a gang of Mexican robbers. On May 11, Governor Bigler approved the act and offered a $1,000 reward for the capture—dead or alive—of any Mexican named Joaquin. To carry out the job, the state hired a group of rangers who were led by Captain Harry Love, a Texas ranger and a veteran of the Mexican-American War (1846–48). Mustered into service on May 17, Love's rangers were given three months to put an end to the violence in California's mining settlements. Charged with capturing five Mexicans by the name of Joaquin, the rangers worked from vague descriptions of the out-

Robin Hood of the West?

Many historians have compared Joaquin Murieta with Robin Hood—a romantic outlaw who stole from the rich and gave to the poor. In his book *Bandits,* Eric Hobsbawm explains, "Such a figure had long existed in men's folk-memories. He was the hero who had sprung spontaneously to life whenever and wherever some people had much and others had nothing. He was, in every land, the man who took from the rich and gave to the poor. He was the Dashing Outlaw, in whose person all might find recklessly displayed their own hidden defiance, their private longings to be something both worse and better than they had it in them to be. In California, in the fantastic early 1850s when he was needed, no such heroic figure existed, but that did not matter. The Forty-niners invented him, and called him by the name of a marauding cattle-thief who did exist—Joaquin Murieta."

laws. Almost any Mexican male was suspect.

The rangers were given three months to carry out their mission. As they neared their deadline, they encountered a group of Mexicans who were camped near the Diablo Range on the Tulare Plains. Following an argument, the rangers killed two of the Mexicans and took the others prisoner. To prove their claim to the reward, the rangers planned to present the governor with the severed heads of the dead Mexicans.

One of the dead men had been so badly disfigured by the gun wound that the rangers severed his hand instead. The hand, missing two fingers, belonged to a man who was later identified as Manuel Garcia, a wanted outlaw known as "Three-Fingered Jack." The rangers beheaded the other man and preserved it in a jar of alcohol. The head was later taken to different towns and put on public display, as proof to the citizens of California that the dangerous Joaquin no longer posed a threat to their safety.

A HEADLESS JOHN DOE

Days later, San Francisco newspapers featured stories boasting the capture of the notorious bandit Joaquin. None, however, mentioned the dead man's last name. It appears that neither the rangers, nor anyone else, knew the true identity of the dead man. To collect the governor's reward, however, the rangers needed to identify the beheaded man. They managed somehow to back up their claim that it was indeed Joaquin Murieta they had killed and they collected their reward.

Opposite page: Posters announced the display of the head of a man named Joaquin, supposedly the notorious bandit Joaquin Murieta.
Reproduced by permission of Getty Images.

WILL BE EXHIBITED

FOR ONE DAY ONLY!

AT THE STOCKTON HOUSE!

THIS DAY, AUG. 12, FROM 9 A. M., UNTIL 6, P. M.

THE HEAD

Of the renowned Bandit!

JOAQUIN!

AND THE

HAND OF THREE FINGERED JACK!

THE NOTORIOUS ROBBER AND MURDERER.

"JOAQUIN" and "THREE-FINGERED JACK" were captured by the *State Rangers*, under the command of Capt. Harry Love, at the Arroya Cantina, July 24th. No reasonable doubt can be entertained in regard to the identification of the head now on exhibition, as being that of the notorious robber, *Joaquin Murietta*, as it has been recognised by hundreds of persons who have formerly seen him.

Will the Real Joaquin Please Stand Up?

Many of the most notable Mexican bandits were named Joaquin—a popular Mexican first name. Notorious bandits Bottellier (or Botilleras), Carrillo, Ocomorenia, and Valenzuela all answered to the name Joaquin.

Within one month of the incident, the press had begun to voice doubts about the true identity of the murdered Mexican. On August 23, 1853, the editor of the *San Francisco Alta* wrote:

> It affords amusement to our citizens … to read the various accounts of the capture and decapitation [beheading] of "the notorious Joaquin Murieta." The humbug [hoax] is so transparent that it is surprising any sensible person can be imposed upon by the statements of the affair which have appeared in the prints. A few weeks ago a party of native Californians and Sonorians started for the Tulare Valley for the expressed and avowed purpose of running mustangs. Three of the party have returned and report that they were attacked by a party of Americans, and that the balance of their party, four in number, had been killed; that Joaquin Valenzuela, one of them, was killed as he was endeavoring to escape, and that his head was cut off by his captors and held as a trophy. It is too well known that Joaquin Murieta was not the person killed by Captain Harry Love's party at the Panoche Pass. The head recently exhibited in Stockton bears no resemblance to that individual, and this is positively asserted by those who have seen the real Murieta and the spurious [fake] head.

HISTORY EMBELLISHED

Historians have not been able to resolve the question of Murieta's fate—whether he died at the hands of the rangers or lived comfortably into old age. This uncertainty did little to discourage biographers and storytellers. The legend of Joaquin Murieta began in earnest in 1854, with the publication of *The Life and Adventures of Joaquin Murieta, Celebrated California Bandit* by John Rollin Ridge. A part-Cherokee journalist, novelist, and poet, Ridge, was known by his Native American pen name, Yellow Bird. His story, which romanticized Murieta's supposed deeds, owed much to the legend of Robin Hood in its treatment of the noble outlaw. Presented as a factual account of the life of Murieta, *The Life and Adventures* provided much of the "history" cited in later accounts.

Over the years Murieta's legend continued to grow as it was rewritten and expanded in books, poems, and a ballad. It even inspired movies. Notable among these is a series of articles written by a young woman reporter and published in the *San Francisco Call* from December 1923 to February 1924. Drawing freely from California legend, the author romanticized Murieta, calling him "The Napoleon of bandits." She described him as commanding some four hundred men and wearing strings of human ears around the horn of his saddle. Later, the celebrated Chilean poet Pablo Neruda wrote a ballad in which Murieta is identified as a heroic Chilean figure. Drawing loosely on the various stories of Murieta, Hollywood writers and directors created legends of such characters as the Cisco Kid and Zorro.

Through the Eyes of a Chilean Poet

Murieta, willful and violent child, return with my song to the metal and mines of your Chile.

All oaths are dissolved, your compass of vengeance comes full circle.

Your land has forgotten you now—the terror you wrought, the poor head under the sickle are shadows that darken a dream. You were one of your country's romantics. —From the Conclusion to *Splendor and Death of Joaquin Murieta* by Pablo Neruda, pp. 173–175

With so many fabulous stories about Murieta, he remains a mystery to historians. It is likely that the facts of his life and death will never be known. He remains important both as a legend and a folk hero—a fictional character who reveals much about the social and cultural climate of California during the exciting years of the California gold rush.

For More Information

Drago, Harry Sinclair. *Road Agents and Train Robbers.* New York: Dodd, Mead, 1973.

Hobsbawm, Eric. *Bandits.* London: Wiedenfeld & Nicolson, 2000, pp. 10, 68, 70, 142, 186.

Jackson, Joseph Henry. *Bad Company.* Lincoln and London: University of Nebraska Press, 1949. Reprint 1977, pp. 3–40, 248, 250, 267.

Lamar, Howard R., ed. *The New Encyclopedia of the American West.* New Haven, CT: Yale University Press, 1988.

Neruda, Pablo. *Splendor and Death of Joaquin Murieta.* Translated by Ben Belitt. New York: Farrar, Straus & Giroux, 1972.

Raymond Patriarca

March 17, 1908
July 11, 1984

Mobster

Patriarca was "just the toughest guy you ever saw."

--A state policeman from Patriarca's native Massachusetts

Some considered Raymond Patriarca to be a fair and "polished" mobster. Others found him to be cruel. No one argues that he ruled New England's underworld for decades and enjoyed ties to the national crime syndicate.

A MAFIOSO ON THE MOVE

Raymond Salvatore Loreda Patriarca was born on Saint Patrick's Day (March 17), 1908, in Worcester, Massachusetts. Three years later, his family moved to Providence, Rhode Island, where his father ran a liquor store. Patriarca left school at the age of eight to work as a shoeshine boy and bellhop. Nothing about his childhood stood out—until 1925, when the seventeen-year-old Patriarca lost his father. He turned to crime and never reversed his path.

The same year his father died, Patriarca was arrested for breaking Prohibition laws (laws forbidding the manufacture, sale, or transfer of alcoholic beverages) in Connecticut. After that he tried his hand at various crimes. He was arrested for breaking and entering, failing to stop for a policeman, and organizing a jail-break, during which a guard and another man were slain. Patriarca worked his way up in the Mafia, an underground organization of criminals who control gambling, drug sales, and other illegal activities in a city or area. He began in a low-level position in Providence and became an associate in the New York Mafia. Soon, he was a full-fledged member of La Cosa Nostra (Italian meaning "Our Thing," another name for the Mafia).

DIRTY POLITICS

During the 1930s the Providence Board of Public Safety named Patriarca Public Enemy Number One. Police were ordered to arrest him on sight. During that time, however, he was imprisoned only once and briefly. In 1938 he was arrested for participating in the robbery of a jewelry store in Brookline, Massachusetts. Convicted of carrying a gun without a permit, carrying burglar's tools, and armed robbery, he was sentenced to three to five years in the state prison. After serving less than three months of that sentence, Patriarca was paroled (released early and under certain conditions). His release prompted an investigation into political corruption inside the office of Governor Charles F. Hurley. In 1941, after three years of investigations, Daniel H. Coakley, a Massachusetts governor's councilor, was removed from office for his role in corrupt political practices.

The Mafia was dominated by "families" of criminals who are loyal to one another. Each family is organized like a business, with each person assigned a certain job and one boss, or don, making the decisions and issuing orders. Already favored by the Genovese and Profaci/Columbo families in New York, Patriarca left prison as a rising star in the New England Mafia. He established many political contacts and was able to gain a powerful stronghold in New England. During the 1940s he was credited as one of the chief movers behind the criminal organization that would become the New England Crime Family.

A FRIENDLY SHARK

A gifted leader and manager, Patriarca had a friendly and polished manner in his dealings with police and the public. He

What Goes Around Comes Around

Joseph "the Animal" Barboza was born in 1932 in New Bedford, Massachusetts. His parents were Portuguese immigrants. As a young boy, he had already run into trouble with the law and spent time in reformatories (institutions where young criminals are confined). In the Mafia, he became a hit man who claimed to have murdered twenty-six men. But by 1966 he had fallen out of favor with his Mafia colleagues. Arrested in October of that year on a concealed weapons charge, he remained in jail for weeks because his mob associates did not come forward to pay his $100,000 bail. After two friends attempted to raise funds for Barboza's bail, they were murdered and dumped in South Boston. The $59,000 they raised vanished with them.

The FBI saw Barboza as a promising informant. By June 1967 they had convinced him to provide evidence against fellow mobsters—many of whom, in his eyes, had turned their backs on him. On June 20, based on Barboza's testimony, Raymond Patriarca and another mobster were indicted on charges of conspiracy to kill Willie Marfeo. Later, the informant's testimony resulted in the indictment of three more mobsters.

In an attempt to silence the former hit man, mobsters planted a bomb in the car of his lawyer, John Fitzgerald. Fitzgerald lost one leg below the knee in the explosion. But Barboza continued to testify. In all, two of the three trials at which he testified resulted in convictions of mobsters.

After Patriarca was convicted, Barboza wrote to the *Boston Herald Traveler* to explain why he had turned against the mob. He was clearly bitter about how he and others had been treated. He wrote:

was respected as a fair leader but feared as a vicious opponent who was ruthless in ordering the murder of anyone who crossed him or posed a threat to his rackets. The 1952 murder of Irish mobster Carlton O'Brien, who threatened Patriarca's leadership of rackets in New England, was one of many killings aimed at strengthening his position.

In 1954 Philip Bucola, the leader of the New England Crime Family since 1946, fled to Sicily. Patriarca moved to the top spot of that criminal empire. With headquarters in Providence, he ran his operation from a two-story frame building. The area soon became an armed camp patrolled by "spotters" who kept an eye out for rivals and police.

"Younger inmates in Walpole and Concord [prisons] would do anything to get in with these people, figuring that they would become big men. The office [Mafia leaders] likes them to believe this because then they bleed every single favorable effort from these disillusioned boys and men—and then throw them a crust of bread…and it goes on and on in one complete cycle of evil and viciousness, while the office sits back, laughs, and reaps the harvest."

In exchange for his testimony, Barboza was granted leniency (a lighter punishment). Sentenced to one year in prison, including time served, he was released in March 1969. He was instructed never to return to Massachusetts. Relocated to California, he was given a new identity. Within a year of his release, however, he committed another killing. In late 1971 he was tried for the murder of an unemployed mechanic. Pleading guilty to a second-degree murder charge, he was sentenced to five years behind bars. While jailed at Folsom Prison in California, he wrote poetry about mob life—and his own bravery.

But Barboza was a marked man. According to reports, the Mafia had put out a $300,000 contract on his life, a hefty reward for anyone who could kill him. Released from prison in October 1975, Barboza began using the name Joe Donati and moved into an inexpensive apartment in San Francisco. But the mob was watching. On February 11, 1976, as he approached his car, he was gunned down by assailants in a white van. The hit made front-page headlines, but few people mourned the mobster's death. Prominent attorney F. Lee Bailey, who sometimes defended Barboza, said, "With all due respect to my former client, I don't think society has suffered a great loss."

"THE ANIMAL" SINGS

Patriarca's influence reached far beyond his stronghold in New England. He is believed to have been a member of the New York Mafia commission, and had secret interests in casinos in Las Vegas and other deals in Florida and Philadelphia. But in 1967 Patriarca's reign ran into a problem. Joseph "The Animal" Barboza, an associate of the New England Crime Family, testified against members of the family in exchange for protection from prosecution and from fellow mobsters. As a result of his testimony, on June 20, Patriarca and two other mobsters were formally charged in federal court for conspiring to murder Willie Marfeo, a Providence bookie (a person who receives and pays off bets), who had been killed the previous year.

Barboza's testimony shook the New England Crime Family. Four mobsters received the death penalty, two drew life sentences—and Patriarca, the head of the family, was sent in March 1969 to a federal prison in Atlanta, Georgia. But he continued to lead the New England mob from behind bars. During that time, he was tried for conspiracy to murder two other men: Marfeo's brother, Rudolph, and Anthony Malei, both of whom were shot to death in Providence on April 20, 1968.

Convicted, Patriarca received a ten-year sentence. After completing his federal sentence in April 1973, he was transferred to a prison in Rhode Island. On January 9, 1975, after serving six years of his sentence, he was granted an early release. Patriarca's parole was issued because of a letter in which Rhode Island's Speaker of the House Joseph Bevilaqua praised the mobster as "a person of integrity [honesty], and, in my opinion, good moral character."

MURDER, HE SAID

Throughout the rest of the 1970s and into the 1980s, Patriarca continued to rule the New England Crime Family. Law enforcement officials tried to gather evidence against him. In 1978, he was accused of being involved in a plot to assassinate (kill for political reasons) Cuban leader Fidel Castro. Fellow mobster Vincent Teresa testified that Patriarca had been present at a meeting in 1960 during which the Central Intelligence Agency (CIA) offered mobsters a $4-million contract to carry out the hit. Teresa further testified that Patriarca had helped choose the hit man—Maurice Werner, a convict from Brookline, Massachusetts. The assassination plot was never attempted.

In 1981 a grand jury in Miami, Florida, officially charged Patriarca with labor racketeering (threatening for profit). In

December 1983 he was charged with arranging the 1965 murder of Raymond "Baby" Curcio, who had burglarized the home of the Patriarca's brother, Joseph. In March of the following year, he was arrested for ordering the 1968 murder of Robert Candos, a bank robber who threatened to testify against him. In spite of his trouble with the law, Patriarca continued to hold on to his power in the New England Crime Family. On July 11, 1984, he died of a heart attack at the home of a girlfriend. He was seventy-six years old.

Former Mafia enforcer Joseph "The Baron" Barboza, center, testified about the connection between infamous mobster Raymond Patriarca and singer/actor Frank Sinatra. *Reproduced by permission of Corbis Corporation.*

For More Information

Kelly, Robert J. *Encyclopedia of Organized Crime in the United States: From Capone's Chicago to the New Urban Underworld.*

Westport, CT: Greenwood Press, 2000, pp. 14–17, 178–180, 237–239.

O'Neill, Gerard, and Dick Lehr. *The Underboss: The Rise and Fall of a Mafia Family.* New York: St. Martin's Press, 1989.

Raymond Loredo Salvatore Patriarca. http://www.geocities.com/Hollywood/Academy/4448/patbio.html (accessed on August 2, 2002).

Rick Porrello's AmericanMafia.com. http://americanmafia.com/Cities/New_England-Boston.html (June 25, 2002).

Sifakis, Carl. *The Encyclopedia of American Crime.* 2d ed. New York: Facts on File, 2001, vol. 2: p. 688.

Torr, James D., ed. *Organized Crime.* San Diego, CA: Greenhaven Press, 1999.

Jonathan Jay Pollard

1954

Spy

While working in Navy intelligence in the 1980s, Jonathan Jay Pollard copied thousands of pages of highly sensitive defense documents for the Israelis. Charged and convicted of espionage, or spying, he is now serving a life sentence.

AN ASPIRING SPY

Born in 1954, Pollard was the youngest of three children. His father was a microbiologist at the prestigious Notre Dame University in South Bend, Indiana. His parents, Jewish-Americans and Zionists (supporters of Israel as a homeland for Jews), taught their children to love Israel, which they considered a Jewish holy land.

A bright student, Pollard was a member of the National Honor Society. After graduating from high school, he attended California's prestigious Stanford University, where he majored in political science. As a college student, Pollard dreamed of becoming a Jewish citizen and joining the Israeli army. He even made up stories about having dual citizenship (a citizen of two

"Assisting the Israelis did not involve or require betraying the United States."

--Jonathon Jay Pollard, in a written statement during his trial

101

Israel's Mossad

Founded before Israel was recognized as an independent nation, the Mossad is an extremely powerful intelligence agency. The leader of the Mossad reports directly to Israel's prime minister, and the agency's large budget is a closely guarded secret. Able to deal with countries with which Israel has no diplomatic ties, the Mossad pursues war criminals and launches missions against Israel's enemies. The agency also supplies Western nations with information about Arab terrorists. It has always worked closely with the CIA. Criticized by some for its tactics, the Mossad sometimes resorts to assassination (killing for political reasons). Agents are staunchly loyal to Israel, and many of the country's top leaders first served in that organization.

countries) and told other students that he was an Israeli agent and member of the Mossad, an Israeli intelligence agency.

After graduating from college, Pollard entered Tufts University in Boston, Massachusetts. There he studied at the highly respected Fletcher School of Law and Diplomacy. He also encountered Uri Ra'Anan, an Israeli scholar and an expert in Soviet affairs. Pollard volunteered to provide the U.S. Central Intelligence Agency (CIA) with information about foreign students at Tufts. In 1977, he approached that agency to ask for a job. But he was refused. By 1979, however, he had worked his way onto the government payroll. He was hired as a civilian, or non-military, employee for the U.S. Navy's Operational Surveillance and Intelligence Center. He later worked for the Naval Intelligence Service.

POLLARD MEETS WITH ISRAELI INTELLIGENCE

While in the Navy, Pollard reportedly met with a great deal of anti-Semitism, or biases against Jews. In 1982 he decided to use his access to classified information to help Israel. His decision was prompted by top-secret orders he discovered, which indicated that Defense Secretary Casper Weinberger intended to pressure Israel to withdraw from Lebanon. According to the United Nations (UN), Israel had invaded Lebanon illegally.

Two years later, Pollard put his plan into action. Through a friend, he arranged to meet Colonel Aviem Sella, a high-level Israeli officer who had fought in four wars and had led the Israeli attack that wiped out Iraq's nuclear reactor. Sella later set up a meeting in Paris, where Pollard met with Yosef Yagur, an Israeli science diplomat who lived in New York, and Raphael Eitan, the leader of an intelligence arm of the Israel Defense

Ministry called Lakam. That organization was so secret that the CIA was not aware of its existence. It gathered confidential information about U.S. policies in the Middle East.

A MOUNTAIN OF TOP-SECRET INFORMATION

Pollard agreed to provide classified information to the Israelis. In exchange, he received $10,000 and a monthly payment of $1,500, which was later increased to $2,500. In 1985 he and his wife were rewarded with a trip to Israel.

Bad Blood

U.S. officials were shocked to discover that Jonathan Pollard had been spying for Israel, a country considered to be a U.S. ally (friendly supporter). In fact, Israel and the United States regularly exchanged information of interest to both countries. After Pollard was convicted of spying, Israel was viewed with suspicion for having betrayed the trust of an ally. Relations between Israel and the United States suffered. Some American Jews began to question their faith in Israel's policies. Others believed that the incident encouraged anti-Semitism (anti-Jewish feelings) in America.

Every other week Pollard delivered documents to the apartment of Irit Erb, a secretary for the Israeli Embassy in Washington, D.C. Once the documents were copied, they were returned to Pollard, who returned them to Naval Intelligence. The copies were passed to Israeli intelligence agencies.

In the end, Pollard smuggled 800 documents and more than 1,000 messages and cables to Israeli intelligence. He supplied the Israelis with top-secret information about weapons systems the United States provided to Israel's Arab enemies; gave them details about Soviet-made arms that were shipped to Arab nations; and passed on electronic communications and information about enemy terrorist headquarters and training camps. With information provided by Pollard, Israel was able to organize an air attack to destroy the Palestinian Liberation Army's headquarters in Tunisia on October 1, 1985. The intelligence Pollard provided allowed Israel's air force to avoid radar detection.

CAUGHT, COOPERATIVE, AND CONFESSING

Pollard's superiors and co-workers began to suspect him of foul play because of the vast number of classified documents he regularly took home. Naval counterintelligence agents began questioning him. Fearing discovery, Pollard and his wife report-

Marion Prison

Most life-term prisoners spend thirty months of their sentence at Marion Prison in Illinois. Some consider Marion to be the worst of all federal penitentiaries. Conditions there are so bad, in fact, that the humanitarian group Amnesty International has protested that the institution is inhumane (cruel). The onetime home to many members of organized crime, including Mafia leader **John Gotti** (see entry), Marion has also housed a number of spies and terrorists. Among those convicted of espionage (spying) were Edwin Wilson, a United States government employee who sold arms to Libya; John Walker, who sold secret information to the Soviet Union; and Jonathan Pollard.

edly called the Israeli embassy in Washington, D.C., to request political asylum (protection). They arrived at the embassy on November 21, 1985, but Israeli security officers refused to allow them in. After no officials came to speak to them, they left. As they drove out of the embassy compound, the Pollards were arrested by U.S. government agents who had been following them.

Both Pollard and his wife, Anne—who had participated in her husband's spying—were charged with espionage. Pollard promised to cooperate with government investigators and willingly confessed that he had been providing Israel with classified documents for seventeen months. He gave them the names of his contacts and listed documents he had provided to Israeli intelligence. Meanwhile, Sella, Erb, and Yagur returned to Israel. Israeli leaders promised to cooperate with the investigation, although some of them denied that Lakam had acted with the government's approval.

THE HIGH PRICE OF TREASON

While Pollard openly admitted to spying, he defended himself by saying that his actions were justified. He claimed that he had spied to help Israel, not to hurt the United States. During the trial, he wrote: "Assisting the Israelis did not involve or require betraying the United States." Further, he claimed that he had provided information about the Soviets and Arabs to "avoid a repetition of the Yom Kippur War," a conflict in 1973–74 that began with a surprise attack on Israel by the Arab countries of Egypt, Syria, and Iraq.

Pollard had no luck convincing the court that his actions had been justified. Casper Weinberger, the U.S. Secretary of Defense, provided U.S. District Court Judge Aubrey Robinson with a long

and detailed memorandum that described Pollard as a danger-ous threat to national security. Weinberger wrote that Pollard "deserved to be hanged or shot" for betraying his country.

In 1987 Pollard was convicted of treason, or betrayal of one's country. He received the maximum sentence: life in a fed-eral penitentiary. It was the harshest sentence ever imposed on a spy for a friendly country. He pleaded that his wife should be treated more gently and claimed that he was responsible for having sacrificed her "on the altar of ideology [ideas]." Anne Pollard was found guilty of collusion (making a secret agree-ment for a dishonest reason) and of abetting, or helping, her husband. She was sentenced to five years in prison. At the time, Pollard was thirty-two years old. His wife was twenty-six. Pol-lard divorced Anne in 1990.

Israeli citizens and Israeli politicians both pleaded with U.S. officials to free Jonathan Pollard after he was sentenced to life in prison for spying on the U.S. for the Israelis. *Reproduced by permission of Corbis Corporation.*

Initially, Israeli officials denied that Pollard had acted with their government's approval. But, pressured by American and Israeli Jews, officials later admitted that the American had acted with the support of the Israeli government. In 1996, Pollard was granted Israeli citizenship.

Two Israeli presidents, several prime ministers, and many American Jews lobbied for Pollard's release. In October 1998, during peace talks with Arab leader Yasser Arafat (1929–) and American President Bill Clinton (1946–), Israeli Prime Minister Binyamin Netanyahu (1949–) held up the discussion to ask to be allowed to take Pollard to Israel. Netanyahu told a *Newsweek* reporter, "It's merely a humanitarian request." He was not the first to ask that Pollard be forgiven. United States presidents Ronald Reagan (1911–) and George [H.W.] Bush (1924–) had already rejected such requests, and Clinton had denied three earlier petitions.

Clinton's top security advisors strongly advised the president not to allow Pollard to leave for Israel or in any way change his sentence. They feared that doing so would send a dangerous message to other nations and would-be spies. Senator Richard Shelby, chairman of the Senate intelligence committee, and Senator Bob Kerrey, the committee's vice chairman, wrote to Clinton. They protested that freeing Pollard would "give credence [weight] to the claim that espionage is somehow less serious when Americans spy on behalf of a friendly nation with which they sympathize." George Tenet, director of the CIA, asserted that he would "find it difficult to remain" at that agency if Clinton were to lessen Pollard's sentence. Joseph diGenova, who prosecuted Pollard, argued that "[h]undreds of millions of dollars had to be spent to correct the damage" done by the American spy, who had provided critical information about sources and methods of U.S. intelligence gathering. Releasing Pollard, diGenova said, "would be a disgrace."

Clinton denied Netanyahu's request. Pollard remains jailed in Butner prison, a low-security federal institution in North Carolina. He once described himself as "a frontline soldier forgotten deep in enemy territory, taking a last stand on a small hill. "

For More Information

Bondi, Victor, ed. *American Decades: 1980–1989*. Detroit, MI: Gale Research, 1996, pp. 338–340.

Kohn, George Childs. *The New Encyclopedia of American Scandal.* New York: Checkmark Books, 2001, pp. 317–318.

Nash, Jay Robert. *Spies: A Narrative Encyclopedia of Dirty Tricks and Double Dealing from Biblical Times to Today.* New York: M. Evans and Company, 1997, pp. 392–393.

Sifakis, Carl. *The Encyclopedia of American Crime.* 2d ed. New York: Facts on File, 2001, vol. 2: pp. 586–587.

Strobel, Brian Duffy, and David Makovsky. "The Spy Who Is Still Stuck in the Cold." *U.S. News & World Report* (January 18, 1999): p. 22.

Thompson, Mark. "America's Traitor, Israel's Patriot." *Time* (November 2, 1998): p. 44.

Watson, Russell. "A Soldier on a Small Hill." *Newsweek* (November 2, 1998): p. 28.

Pretty Boy Floyd

(Charles Arthur Floyd)

February 3, 1901
October 22, 1934

AKA: Jack Hamilton

Robber, Murderer

"I never shot at a fellow in my life unless I was forced into it by some trap and then it was that or else."

--Charles "Pretty Boy" Floyd, in a letter to Vivian Brown, a reporter for the *Oklahoma News*

Reproduced by permission of Getty Images.

In the 1930s Pretty Boy Floyd emerged as an American folk hero, but the Federal Bureau of Investigation (FBI) believed he was a key figure in a Kansas City massacre that claimed five lives, including FBI agents and gangster Frank "Jelly" Nash. Floyd fiercely denied having taken part in the killings and his involvement was never proved. The popular outlaw died following a shoot-out with FBI agents. Some claimed it was an execution-style slaying.

THE MAGNIFICENT FLOYDS

Charles Arthur Floyd was born on February 3, 1901, in the Cookson Hills of Oklahoma, an area that had once been part of the Cherokee Nation. His father, Walter Floyd was a hardworking and generous man but was reportedly a stern guardian, as was his religious mother, Mamie Echols.

With eight children to feed, the Floyds enjoyed few luxuries. After trying to farm cotton in Hanson, Oklahoma, Walter moved his family to a farm in Sequoyah County, near

Akins. As sharecroppers, the Floyds rented land to grow fruits and vegetables. They also raised chickens, hogs, and cows.

Eventually Walter put together enough money to open a general store in Akins. With the additional income, the family lived more comfortably than many of their neighbors. Hardworking and honest, the Floyds enjoyed an excellent reputation throughout the county. Walter Floyd was an upstanding member of the local Baptist church, and the family read the Bible together before bedtime.

Never an enthusiastic student, Charles Floyd left school after finishing the sixth grade. Ruby Hardgraves, who later became his wife, recalled, "When we were kids, Charles was the school hero. He wasn't studious, he was too busy laughing." Floyd left school with a basic education: He could read, write, and do simple math.

Although he was generally considered a good boy, Floyd had a reputation for devilish behavior. Some suspected that he was guilty of a number of small thefts in the area. J. H. Harkrider, a local merchant, later recalled:

> I guess the first thing Pretty Boy Floyd ever stole was from my grocery store. I had some little cakes in boxes and they kept disappearing. I marked some boxes and watched to see where they went. He was just a kid at that time, and came in the store and stood around and left. I counted the boxes and one was missing. I got an officer and we went around to the [alley] and he was there eating some cookies. I asked him where he got the cookies and he admitted getting them out of my store, after I showed him the mark. We tried to scare him up and show him he couldn't steal, and let him go.

Don't Call Him Pretty Boy

Floyd reportedly did not like the nickname Pretty Boy. Around his hometown people called him Charlie or Chock, after the name of a beer he enjoyed. But after leaving home he was dubbed Pretty Boy. According to legend, the name was a reference to his fine clothes and well-groomed hair. The gangster refused to acknowledge the nickname to his dying day. As the story goes, when FBI agents asked the mortally wounded outlaw whether he was indeed Pretty Boy, he responded, "I'm Charles Arthur Floyd."

From box houses to the Big House

At age twenty, Floyd married Ruby Hardgraves, his childhood sweetheart. She was sixteen. After a boom period, Oklahoma was then suffering an economic downturn. Cotton, oil, and other prices plummeted. Jobs were scarce. Young and inexperienced, Floyd had a difficult time finding work. In search of employment, he soon left home.

"Charlie eventually joined the lumpen migrant class [a group of workers who travel from place to place in search of jobs] that drifted away to smelters [metal workers], mines and oil fields," author Dan Morgan described in the *Washington Post*. "Even in the best of times, the mining and smelter towns were dangerous, polluted, unhealthy places, sorely lacking in basic services and functioning institutions—more camps than communities. Few houses had indoor toilets, and water was delivered by wagon. People made their own "box houses" out of used lumber with old newspapers for wallpaper."

Frustrated with his attempts to make an honest living, Floyd got a pistol. In 1925, his wife then pregnant, he took a train to St. Louis, Missouri, where he robbed a payroll of $5,000. Caught shortly after the robbery, he was tried, convicted, and sentenced to three years in the Missouri State Penitentiary. Charles Hargus, the assistant deputy warden at the penitentiary, later described his impression of the young Oklahoman:

> I doubt if Floyd was a wanton killer. He would shoot and shoot to kill when cornered, but he didn't impress me as the type who would slay a man for the pleasure of killing. That doesn't mean that he was a model prisoner. He would steal things, like most of the convicts, but he didn't go out of his way to hunt trouble.

Floyd was released after serving only part of his sentence. He returned home to Oklahoma. But prison had changed him.

From bad to worse

At the time of Floyd's release, Oklahoma was still in the midst of an economic crisis. That, together with his criminal record, made it nearly impossible to find honest work. In correspondence with *Oklahoma News* reporter Vivian Brown, Floyd wrote:

The Bloodiest 47 Acres of America

In 1925 Floyd was sentenced to three years in the Missouri State Penitentiary, also known as Jeff City because it is located in Jefferson, Missouri. When he was released after serving half of his sentence, he reportedly vowed never to step foot in prison again.

Established in 1836, Jeff City is one of the oldest prisons in the nation and was the first prison west of the Mississippi River. With three thousand inmates when Floyd entered in 1925, the penitentiary was growing at an alarming rate. Although its property had grown from 4 to 47 acres, the jail could not accommodate the thousands of prisoners who were sentenced to do time at what became known as "the bloodiest 47 acres of America." Cells that were built for one person were occupied by two. By the time Floyd was released, the prison population had increased to four thousand. Jeff City housed about 80 percent more inmates than the institution was designed to hold.

In spite of reforms, Jeff City was a brutal environment. Untrained guards imposed strict discipline on the inmates, who were frequently subjected to whippings, sweat treatments, cold baths, and other punishments. Prisoners worked twelve-hour days, walking to their job assignments with their ankles bound. Meals, clothing, and medical care were barely adequate.

By all accounts, Charles Floyd left Missouri State Penitentiary a changed man. Hardened to the violence he had seen, plagued by his criminal record, and acquainted with experienced criminals, he soon returned to a life of crime. Nevertheless, he kept his vow, and never returned to prison during his life.

I was just a green country kid that got caught on a job [robbery], but I guess that was the job that put its mark on me and I could never shake it off. Yes, I tried.

After I got out of serving time in Jeff City, I really didn't [figure] to go on with life of that kind, but every place I went they [law enforcement officers] picked me up.

I finally went to Colorado and was looking for a job in Pueblo when they picked me up as a vag [a vagrant—with no money] and gave me 60 days.

When I got out I went to Kansas City and the second day there they got me again. Then I went to Ohio and was picked up in Akron and later in Toledo.

I couldn't shake those guys off [no] matter where I went. I went back to K.C. and met Bill Miller [another bank robber]. By then, I decided I'd just as well get the goods as have the name, and once you get started in this game you can't turn back.

I guess after I went back to Kansas City I did go from bad to worse. I knew I could never live with my wife and kid and make a decent living, and that sure gets a fellow.

Moving eastward, Floyd pulled a number of bank heists alone and with other professionals. In 1930, he was arrested and convicted for robbing a bank in Sylvania, Ohio. Sentenced to 10 to 25 years in the Ohio State Penitentiary, he managed to escape on his way to prison. Just 10 miles (16 kilometers) from the prison gates, he jumped through a train window, rolled down a hill, and ran.

Floyd returned to Kansas City and looked up Bill Miller, a younger bank robber, also on the run from the cops, who had been recommended as trustworthy. Starting with small robberies, the pair worked their way up to bank heists. After striking a number of banks in northern Michigan, they returned to St. Louis, where they met Rose Ash and Beulah Bird in a brothel. After reportedly killing their husbands, Floyd and Miller took the two women on the road with them. In Kentucky, they launched another bank-robbing campaign, hitting banks in Mt. Zion, Elliston, and Whitehouse.

Returning to Ohio, the foursome paused in Bowling Green to enjoy the spoils of their robberies. Their presence did not go unnoticed. A shoot-out with law enforcement left Police Chief Carl Galligher dead and another officer wounded. Bill Miller was also killed and both women were wounded.

ROBIN HOOD OF COOKSON HILLS

Floyd returned to Oklahoma, where he hooked up with a former church deacon named George Birdwell. Together they robbed banks throughout the Southwest. Hiding in his native territory, Floyd took on a reputation as the "Robin Hood of Cookson Hills."

"Banks were unloved institutions in those days, responsible for foreclosing on farmers and losing people's savings," explains author Dan Morgan. "Not only outlaws but ordinary citizens robbed banks in eastern Oklahoma." Guards and local law enforcement officials were often unreliable because many of them shared this distrust of banks.

But Floyd did more than steal money. While robbing a bank, he often destroyed first mortgages in the hopes that they had not yet been recorded. Without any record of the loan, the bank could not foreclose, or take over a farm, when the farmers fell on hard times. It was also reported that he sometimes threw fistfuls of money at children. "It was all bonded money," he later explained to *Oklahoma News* reporter Vivian Brown, "and no one ever lost anything except the big boys." Elsewhere, he wrote, "I have robbed no one but monied men."

THEY'RE NOT IN KANSAS CITY ANYMORE

On June 17, 1933, a squad of police officers were ambushed as they escorted Frank "Jelly" Nash from a train into a car at Union Station, in Kansas City, Missouri. Four law officers died in the shoot-out and two were wounded. Also killed in the shooting was gangster Frank Nash.

Floyd's involvement in that incident was never proved. Police also were not able to figure out the motive for the crime. At first it was assumed that the killings occurred during a botched attempt to free Nash from his captors. But in 1954 a mob informer named Blackie Audett told a different story. Audett, who claimed to have witnessed the incident, identified the gunmen as Vern Miller, Maurice Denning, and William "Solly" Weisman. He also claimed to have known in advance about the shooting. He said it was arranged as a hit on Nash, who knew too much about the city government's links to organized crime. A third theory about the massacre involves an FBI cover-up, in which one of the law agents killed Nash and fellow officers when his shotgun misfired.

Pretty Boy Floyd always denied his involvement in the Kansas City massacre which left cars riddled with bullet holes and five policemen and mobster Frank Nash dead. *Reproduced by permission of Corbis Corporation.*

Although witnesses to the killings did not immediately identify Floyd as one of the shooters, he was later identified by name. On June 21, 1933, he wrote a postcard to Kansas City Detective Captain Thomas J. Higgins. The card read:

Dear Sirs:

I—Charles Floyd—want it made known that I did not participate in the massacre of officers at Kansas City.

[signed]Charles Floyd

Floyd's protests were useless. FBI Director Herbert Hoover identified him as one of the shooters, and labeled him Public Enemy Number One. His days were numbered.

DEAD AND BURIED

Historians are divided as to whether Floyd was involved in the massacre. Whether guilty or not, the incident set off a manhunt for the fugitive Okla-homan. On October 22, 1934, FBI agents caught up with Floyd on a farm in Ohio. As he ran for cover in the cornfields, he was felled by gunfire. The FBI agents, including Melvin Purvis, reported that Floyd died then and there.

Rumors about Floyd's death soon began to circulate. According to one story, Floyd had only been wounded in the cornfield and was later executed by agents who were eager to kill Public Enemy Number One. Forty years after the incident, Chester Smith, a local lawman who had been involved in the manhunt, confirmed this story. He claimed that he had not come forward sooner because he was afraid to disagree with the FBI's story. The circumstances of Floyd's death, like the question of his involvement in the Kansas City massacre, may never be known.

Newspapers reported Floyd's death in a dramatic style typical of the times: He was described by one Texas paper as an "infamous outlaw whose bullets blazed a crimson path over a dozen Midwestern states." In spite of having been condemned by the FBI and the national press, Floyd remained a heroic robber to many people. An estimated crowd of ten thousand attended his funeral. Many of them attempted to take souvenirs from the site.

What Have I Done to Deserve This?

Floyd's acquaintance Adam Richetti was also accused of participating in the Kansas City massacre. Like Floyd, he strongly denied having been involved—right up to his dying day. He was charged, tried, and convicted for his suspected role in the massacre and on October 7, 1938, Richetti was executed at the Missouri State Penitentiary in Jefferson City. As he was escorted to the gas chamber, he again denied any involvement in the Kansas City incident, pleading, "What have I done to deserve this?"

For More Information

Charles "Pretty Boy" Floyd. http://www.geocities.com/Capitol Hill/Lobby/3935/ (accessed on August 2, 2002).

Grogan, David. "Homage to an Outlaw." *People* (July 6, 1992).

Helmer, William, and Rick Mattix. *Public Enemies: America's Criminal Past, 1919–1940.* New York: Checkmark Books, 1998.

King, Jeffery S. *The Life and Death of Pretty Boy Floyd.* Kent, OH: Kent State University, 1998.

Nash, Jay Robert. *Bloodletters and Badmen*. 1973. Abridged. New York: Warner Paperback Library, 1975, book 2: pp. 179–186, 212–218.

Prassel, Frank Richard. *The Great American Outlaw: A Legacy of Fact and Fiction*. Norman, OK: University of Oklahoma Press, 1993, p. 275.

Sifakis, Carl. *The Encyclopedia of American Crime*. 2d ed. New York: Facts on File, 2001, pp. 320–322, 478–479, 602.

Eric Robert Rudolph

1966 or 1967

Suspected Terrorist and Murderer

Wanted in connection with the 1996 bombing at the Olympic Games in Atlanta, Georgia, and abortion clinic bombings in Atlanta as well as Birmingham, Alabama, Eric Robert Rudolph has managed to avoid capture. Authorities believe he has used his skills as a survivalist to hide out in an isolated "no-man's land" in the rugged Appalachian Mountains in North Carolina.

"THERE IS A BOMB IN CENTENNIAL PARK"

In July and August 1996, the twenty-sixth Summer Olympic Games were being held in Atlanta, Georgia. Promising to break attendance records, the Games were the first to be hosted by an American city since the 1984 Summer Olympics were staged in Los Angeles, California. But on July 27, 1996—the first Saturday of the Games—something happened that would cast a shadow over the international sporting event and provide a wake-up call for the coordinators of future Olympics. At about 1:20 in the morning, a bomb exploded in Centennial Olympic Park in downtown Atlanta, killing one person and injuring more than one hundred others.

"If Eric Rudolph is in these mountains, they ain't going to find him."

--A resident of Rudolph's home town in North Carolina, quoted in *Time* magazine

Another Olympic Casualty

Although the Atlanta bombing in July 1996 officially claimed only one casualty, a second death was attributed to the explosion. Melih Uzanyol, a Turkish cameraman, attempted to capture the aftermath of the bombing on tape. He died from a fatal heart attack he suffered while taping.

Authorities had been warned about the bomb, but with little time to act. Just twenty minutes before the explosion, a man who did not identify himself called the emergency number 911 to say "There is a bomb in Centennial Park." With no further explanation, he added "You have thirty minutes." The call was placed at 1:06 a.m., from a telephone a few blocks away from the park.

Minutes earlier, a security guard who was patrolling a concert in the park noticed an abandoned green knapsack. The guard informed a police officer that he had seen the bag near a tower across from the stage. After the officer checked the bag, he contacted bomb specialists to determine whether the contents were, in fact, deadly.

Two men who were already in Centennial Park—an agent from the Federal Bureau of Investigation (FBI) and another from the Bureau of Alcohol, Tobacco, and Firearms (ATF)—took a look at the bag's contents. After they noticed wires and pipes inside the knapsack, at about 1:15 a.m., they began to clear the area. Georgia State troopers helped move people out of the park and away from what was believed to be a bomb. Richard Jewell, the guard who had first spotted the knapsack, had also begun to usher people away from the area.

THE WRONG SUSPECT

When the 40-pound (18-kilogram) bomb detonated, it shot shrapnel (pieces of metal) as far as 100 feet (30 meters). The explosion killed Alice Hawthorne, a forty-three-year-old African American businesswoman, and wounded 111 others. Officials believe that many other people would have been killed or injured had Jewell not taken the initiative to rally other security guards to escort people out of the area. First hailed as a hero, Jewell later became the FBI's chief suspect.

After months of interrogation and investigation, the FBI found nothing to link Jewell to the bombing. In October 1996, the U.S. Department of Justice announced that he was no longer viewed as a suspect. By the end of the year, the FBI asked for the public's help to identify the person responsible for the bombing. They made public the audio tape of the 911 call and circulated a picture of a knapsack like the one found in Centennial Park. The FBI also posted a $500,000 reward for information leading to the arrest and conviction of the terrorist. But the identity of the bomber or bombers remained a mystery—as did the reason for the bombing.

A GRAY TRUCK OFFERS A CLUE

Not long after the Centennial Park explosion, two more bombings rocked the Atlanta area. On January 16, 1997, a bomb detonated at a family planning clinic, injuring six people. That same year, another bomb went off in a gay nightclub. The two bombings had some things in common. Both bombs relied on Westclox timers. And both were backed up by a second bomb containing nails. The second bombs were set to go off at a later time—after the police arrived.

The FBI struggled to piece together what little information they had. Eventually they arrived at a suspect: a thirty-one-year-old North Carolina native named Eric Robert Rudolph, whose gray Nissan pickup truck had been seen leaving the scene of the nightclub bombing. "The witness had reportedly seen a man wearing a blond wig get into a truck and drive away. After tracing the license number," *People* reported, "police identified Rudolph as a suspect and focused their search on western North Carolina, where they found the abandoned truck nine days later. Near the pickup, [deputy police chief] Cooley says, police found strands of fake blond hair. They also discovered a shovel with soil samples matching the dirt in which the bomb had been planted under a flowerpot." The manhunt for Rudolph began and investigators remained tight-lipped, even to this day, about the evidence allegedly linking Rudolph to the blasts in Atlanta.

EVIDENCE OF A SERIAL BOMBER

On January 19, 1998, a Birmingham, Alabama abortion clinic was bombed, killing thirty-four-year-old Robert Sander-

Olympic Terrorists

On July 27, 1996, a bomb exploded in the heart of Olympic festivities in a park in downtown Atlanta, Georgia. It was the first act of terrorism directed at the Olympic Games since the 1972 Summer Games in Munich, Germany, where eleven Israeli athletes were killed by members of Black September, a Palestinian guerrilla group. The terrorists planned the attack to call attention to their demand for the release of Arab guerrillas jailed in Israel.

son, a police officer who was moonlighting as a security guard. The clinic's forty-one-year-old head nurse, Emily Lyons, was injured; she lost an eye and received other wounds as the result of the blast.

Lab reports confirmed that the Birmingham clinic bomb and the bomb planted in the Atlanta nightclub were similar in both design and makeup. The FBI began to uncover evidence that

Rudolph—whose truck sighting made him a prime suspect in the nightclub bombing—was involved in the Birmingham attack as well.

A storage shed Rudolph (a part-time carpenter) rented near Murphy, North Carolina, yielded flooring nails identical to those used in both the Atlanta nightclub and Birmingham clinic bombings. Both bombs contained steel plates that were designed to spray shrapnel. The steel in the plates came from a North Carolina metalworking plant where one of Rudolph's friends happened to work.

The Christian Identity Group

Nord Davis, a native of Cherokee County, North Carolina—where Rudolph lived for seventeen years—led an extremist group called Northpoint Tactical Teams. Davis taught his followers the Christian Identity dogma, a belief system that promoted racism and anti-Semitism (anti-Jewish views). Mark Potok, a spokesperson for the Southern Law Poverty Center, which tracks hate groups, summarized his organization's findings: Christian Identity followers believe that Jews are Satan's children and are planning to create one world government. They also believe that white people are God's chosen people and that all people of color—whom they hatefully refer to as "mud people"—are inferior. Davis died in September 1997, but his teachings appeared to live on. Bigoted, racist, armed and dangerous, Rudolph has been identified as a follower of Davis and the Christian Identity group.

LEAST TOLERANT, MOST WANTED

Shortly after the Birmingham bombing, Eric Robert Rudolph disappeared, probably into the backwoods of the southern Appalachian Mountains. A former private in the 101st Airborne division, he trained to be a highly skilled survivalist. He was also known as an extremist, a person whose bigoted views were evident early in life. As a student at Nantahala School in North Carolina, he once wrote a paper claiming that the Nazi Holocaust—responsible for the deaths of thousands of Jewish people during World War II (1939–45)—was a myth. Investigators also uncovered evidence that the adult Rudolph was a follower of the Christian Identity movement, whose members believe in white supremacy and condemn abortion.

The FBI named Rudolph as a primary suspect in the Birmingham bombing and offered a $100,000 reward for information leading to his capture and conviction. Rudolph was also placed on the FBI's Most Wanted list. A manhunt covered territory from North Carolina to Colorado.

A FUGITIVE SIGHTING

Not seen since the day after the Birmingham bombing in January 1998, Rudolph surfaced in North Carolina that July. He was seen buying large quantities of trail mix, batteries, raisins, burgers and fries from Burger King, and a *Krull the Conqueror* video. On July 7, he showed up at the home of George Nordmann, the owner of a health food store in Andrews, North Carolina, not far from the fugitive's hometown of Murphy.

Rudolph looked very different. He claimed to have lost 6 inches (15 centimeters) from his waistline because he had been eating nothing more than green bananas and oatmeal. He had also grown a beard and long hair, which he wore in a ponytail. Rudolph tried to convince Nordmann that he was not guilty of the bombings. After about thirty minutes, he left. He later returned, when Nordmann was absent, and collected about seventy-five pounds of food, including cans of tuna fish, beets, corn, and green beans. Leaving $500 in Nordmann's house, he fled in the store owner's 1977 Nissan pickup truck, which was later found abandoned at a campground.

Overcome by guilt for harboring a possible terrorist, Nordmann informed authorities that he had seen Rudolph. The manhunt in the mountains of southwest North Carolina intensified, but to no avail. "If Eric Rudolph is in these mountains, they ain't going to find him," a local resident told *Time*. "He's from here," she continued. "I'd never turn him in for a million dollars and then have to live with it the rest of my life." As of early 2002, Rudolph had not been captured. If found and convicted, he could be sentenced to death.

For More Information

Gottesman, Ronald, ed. *Violence in America: An Encyclopedia.* New York: Charles Scribner's Sons, 1999, vol. 1: p. 27, pp. 140–141, 159–160.

FBI Ten Most Wanted Fugitive. http://www.fbi.gov/mostwant/ topten/fugitives/rudolph.htm (accessed on August 2, 2002).

Johnson, Kevin. "The FBI's Most Hunted: List Marks Half-Century." *USA Today* (March 14, 2000).

"Milestones." *Time International* (November 27, 2000).

Monroe, Sylvester. "The Forest Is His Ally: A Fugitive Reappears, Only to Slink Back into the Woods—Among Those for Whom He Is Almost a Hero." *Time* (July 27, 1998).

Reeves, Jay. "Army of God Says It Bombed Clinic." *San Antonio Express-News* (February 3, 1998).

Rhee, Foon, and Diane Suchetka. "Western N.C.: Where Extremists Find a Home." *Charlotte Observer* (February 16, 1998).

Sifakis, Carl. *The Encyclopedia of American Crime.* 2d ed. New York: Facts on File, 2001, vol. 1: pp. 44–45.

Pamela Smart

May 1, 1990
AKA: Maiden of Metal
Murderer

"I thought there were two options: I would be found not guilty, or there would be a hung jury. I never thought this would become a reality."

--Pamela Smart, quoted in *Ladies Home Journal*

Days before her first wedding anniversary, Pamela Smart had her teenage lover, Billy Flynn, murder her twenty-four-year old husband, Greg Smart. Flynn and two friends ambushed and shot Greg in his home, as he returned from work. They tried to make the murder look like a botched burglary. Chillingly, Pamela Smart had told her teenage lover to put her dog in the basement so that it would not be traumatized by the murder. Smart was sentenced to life with no chance of parole for being an accomplice to first-degree murder, conspiring to murder, and witness tampering.

A LOVABLE, FRIENDLY MAIDEN OF METAL

John and Linda Wojas moved their three children from Miami, Florida, to New Hampshire when their daughter, Pamela, was eight years old. Her parents later recalled nothing that would have indicated her future. "We try to think back through all her childhood years, if we could ever see a mean streak in her," her father told *People* magazine. "She was the most lovable, friendly kid."

At Pinkerton Academy, Pam Wojas was an honor student and class officer. She was well-liked by other students, was a member of the school's cheerleading squad, and dated the captain of the football team. After graduating from high school, she enrolled in Florida State University, where she was disc jockey for a weekly college radio show called *Metal Madness*. A devoted fan of heavy metal performers such as Van Halen, Mötley Crüe, and Bon Jovi, she called herself the Maiden of Metal.

A PERFECT COUPLE?

Pam Wojas met Greg Smart during her Christmas break in 1985. At the time, Smart was living at home, working in construction and automobile body repair. According to the couple's friends and family, Wojas aggressively pursued him from the start. He shared her enthusiasm for hard rock music and partying. And she thought that he looked like her rock-and-roll idol, Jon Bon Jovi.

During Wojas's final year in college, Smart moved to Florida to be with her. After she graduated in 1988, they returned to New Hampshire, where he landed a job working for the national insurance firm where his father was employed. The couple moved into an attractive new condominium in a Derry, New Hampshire, complex, just two blocks from where Smart's parents lived. On May 7, 1989, Pam Wojas and Greg Smart were married in the Lowell, Massachusetts, church where his parents, John and Linda Smart, had been wed thirty years earlier.

WORKING FOR A LIVING

Pam Smart worked as a media-services director for the regional school district in Hampton, New Hampshire, where she was in charge of publishing a newsletter and overseeing press relations for Hampton's eleven schools. She also conducted video workshops for students.

Greg was a natural salesman and excelled at his job at the insurance firm. He worked long hours, won office awards, and was appointed rookie of the year. He cut his hair shorter and cut back on partying. Pam did not approve of the changes in her husband. "She didn't want to see Greg turn into a yuppie," Greg's mother, Judy Smart, later explained to *People* magazine. "She wanted him to keep his hair long, to party on weekends with their friends. But Greg had gotten past that point. He wasn't this rock star [Bon Jovi] she was talking about all the time."

YOUNG LOVE

In the fall of 1989, a few months after she was married, Pam met fifteen-year old Billy Flynn at Winna High School, where both were participating in a training session for a drug-awareness program. "She told me she had been a deejay in Florida," Flynn later told *Ladies Home Journal*. "She said she'd had backstage passes and met Mötley Crüe and Van Halen. That's my favorite group." Soon, the two became involved in a sexual relationship, meeting in her office, her car, and eventually, her condominium. When Greg was away on business trips, Pam invited her young lover to stay overnight in her home.

Flynn, whose father had died three years earlier in a car crash, was flattered by the attention from an older woman. He later testified (quoted in *People*), "I was shocked. It's not every day that a 15-year-old kid gets this 22-year-old woman who is very attractive to say that she likes him."

Eventually, Pam began to complain to Flynn that her husband verbally abused and beat her. She showed him bruises on her body, claiming that Greg was responsible, and explained that she had to run into the street in her nightgown to escape from him. She also said she was afraid that Greg would leave her with nothing if she divorced him.

MUST HAVE MISPLACED THE "WIDOW'S HANDBOOK"

On May 1, one week before Greg and Pam Smart's first wedding anniversary, he returned home from sales calls around 9 p.m. When Pam later returned home from a school board meeting, she found her husband's body in the foyer of their condominium. He had been killed by a single gunshot to the back of the head. Pam ran from door to door, informing neighbors of the killing. Soon, Greg's parents and police arrived. The Smarts were devastated by their son's murder. But observers noted that Pam displayed no emotion.

The murder looked like a robbery gone bad. The apartment had been torn apart, and Pam Smart informed police that almost $300 in jewelry was missing, as were a number of CDs. But investigators were suspicious. The crime simply did not fit the profile of a typical burglary. The "burglars" struck during the evening, when people were likely to be home; they chose an apartment easily seen by neighbors; and they carried a gun. "Burglars don't usually carry guns," Derry police Captain Loring

Cold-Blooded

"In my life and 25 years experience in the insurance business, I have never met such a cold person." —Bill Smart, Greg's father, quoted in *People*

Jackson told *Ladies Home Journal,* "and they don't usually work high-density condos, where they are likely to be spotted. Red flags were going up for us immediately."

The young widow's behavior shocked friends and relatives. She wore hot pink to her husband's wake. Just two days after Greg Smart's murder, Pam contacted WMUR-TV reporter Bill Spencer to ask him to interview her. Again, she wore a hot-pink dress and gaudy jewelry. In a matter of weeks she began carousing at nightclubs. Later, she defended her behavior. "I'm sorry if I reacted wrong [to Greg's death]," she said after her trial, quoted in *Ladies Home Journal,* "but nobody gave me the twenty-two-year-old widow's handbook."

BLACK WIDOW

On June 10, about one month after the murder, Vance Lattime Sr. turned in some of his revolvers to police. His son Ralph had heard his other son Vance Jr.—a very close friend of Billy Flynn—discussing his involvement with Flynn in a homicide. Vance Sr. believed his revolver might have been used as the murder weapon. After he turned his collection over to police they determined that his .38-caliber Charter Arms revolver had been used to kill Greg Smart.

That same day Billy Flynn and his friends Patrick Randall, seventeen, and Vance Lattime, eighteen, were arrested and charged with murder. They told police how they had killed Greg Smart. They also told them why—Pam Smart wanted her husband dead.

The teens also revealed Smart's role in planning her husband's murder. She instructed them to enter her condominium through the basement door and to shut her dog, named Halen after the rock star, in the basement so that he would not be traumatized. Flynn, Randall, and Lattime described the killing in detail. They wore dark clothes and latex gloves with scotch tape on their fingertips to avoid leaving fingerprints. They entered the condominium just after dark, and waited for Greg until he arrived home around 9 p.m. They jumped him and wrestled him to the floor.

Randall, who was supposed to slit Greg's throat with a butcher knife, could not bring himself to do it. The teens demanded that Greg hand over his wedding ring. He refused. Randall later testified, "He said his wife would kill him." Next Flynn put a gun to Greg's head. "A hundred years it seemed like," he later testified. "And I said, 'God forgive me'.... I pulled the trigger." Flynn and Randall, certified as adults, received forty years in jail and Lattime got thirty years.

NO ONE WINKED

Police wanted evidence to prove beyond a shadow of a doubt that Pam Smart was involved in her husband's murder. Cecilia Pierce, a friend of both Smart and the teens, provided that evidence. On July 13, police sent Pierce, who was wearing a recording device, to talk to Smart. The two women had previously agreed that if Pierce were asked to wear a wire, she would let Smart know by winking. "For a few minutes I had to think to myself, 'Should I wink?,'" Pierce told *People*. "But I didn't wink, and she told all." Police believed that Smart had her husband killed in order to collect his life insurance. At the time of her arrest, she had been paid $90,000 of the $140,000 policy—of which she had spent nearly half.

WISHING HER A LONG LIFE

Pam Smart's murder trial was held in Rockingham County Superior Court in Exeter, New Hampshire. In televised proceedings that lasted two weeks, a jury of seven men and five women heard the case. The trial made headlines around the world.

Smart claimed she was innocent throughout. Defense attorneys attempted to portray the teens as "deranged thrill killers" who murdered Greg Smart in order to eliminate Flynn's romantic rival. But prosecuting attorneys argued that Pam had coldly and deliberately plotted her husband's murder. Prosecutor Paul Maggiotto (quoted in *Time*), claimed that "she got her hooks so deep in the hormones" of Billy Flynn that the teen could not refuse her request.

Cecilia Pierce, whose conversation with Smart was played in court, was the prosecution's star witness. When Smart took the

Witness for the Prosecution

Sixteen-year-old Cecilia Pierce knew that Pam Smart had plotted her husband's murder. At first, she felt uneasy about helping police collect evidence against her friend by wearing a recording device. But she put those doubts aside. "It was really bothering me that Pam had her husband killed. Her lover was in jail, and she didn't care. And how was I supposed to believe that she was actually my friend? I could hang myself knowing what I know, and she'd be relieved because that's one less person who could tell."

Pierce's instincts about her "friendship" with Smart proved true. After she was imprisoned, Smart was charged with trying to arrange to have Pierce killed by another inmate.

stand, she did little to help her own case. Few believed her claim that her conversation with Pierce was really part of her own investigation into her husband's murder.

After deliberating for thirteen hours, the jury found Pamela Smart guilty of being an accomplice to first-degree murder, conspiracy to commit murder, and tampering with a witness. Judge Douglas R. Gray delivered the mandatory sentence—life in prison with no possibility of parole. "I think life in prison without the possibility of parole for this young lady is very fitting," Captain Loring Jackson told *People*. "I wish her a long life."

For More Information

"Convict Accuses Inmates of Assault." *Buffalo News* (November 10, 1997).

Fitzgerald, Jim. "Smart Testifies She Still Wears Wedding Ring." *Buffalo News* (December 4, 1997).

Gibbs, Nancy. "Murders They Wrote; Passion, Envy and Genius Combine in a Trio of True-Life Crime Dramas That Seem Ready-Made for TV." *Time* (April 1, 1991).

Hanchett, Doug. "Killer Wife Trying to Get Smart with a College Degree." *Boston Herald* (November 30, 1999).

Heaney, Joe. "Smart Back in Jail as Judge Nixes 'Unjust' Bid." *Boston Herald* (June 14, 1997).

"The Hunt Is On for Scheming Helen." *Daily Record (Glasgow, Scotland)* (March 6, 1999).

"Jury Convicts 2 of Beating Pamela Smart in Prison." *Buffalo News* (December 5, 1997).

"Pam Smart 'Merciful' to Attackers." *Boston Herald* (January 8, 1998).

"Pamela Smart Brings Assault Charges." *Los Angeles Times* (November 10, 1997).

Plummer, William. "Grieving Spouse or Black Widow? Police Say Pamela Smart Had Her 16-Year-Old Lover Murder Her Husband." *People* (February 4, 1991).

Sawicki, Stephen. "School Aide Pam Smart Coaxed Her Student Lover to Kill Her Husband—Only to Receive a Lesson in Justice." *People* (April 8, 1991).

"Smart Conspirator Seeks N.H. Pardon." *Boston Herald* (June 7, 2000).

Wright, Rosalind. "The Temptress Bride." *Ladies Home Journal* (July 1991).

David Smith

1969
Computer Criminal

"Imagine if all the germs and the diseases of the world were invented by people and not by nature. Imagine how disgusting that would be."

--David Pottruck, quoted in *Network World*

David L. Smith was a network programmer when he pirated, or broke into and stole, an America Online account and unleashed a macro virus, called Melissa, that disrupted operations for as many as one million computer users. His stunt is thought to have cost affected organizations as much as $393 million in damages. After an investigation that lasted only days, Smith was caught and charged with interruption of public communication. Variants of the Melissa virus are still spreading.

A BANKRUPT COMPUTER GEEK

David Smith grew up in Matawan, New Jersey. During the 1990s, he lived in several cities in south Florida, where he worked at a computer firm. After losing his job, he used his credit card to put off paying bills and soon accumulated $23,860 in credit card debt.

After filing for bankruptcy in 1996, Smith moved back to New Jersey to live with his parents. Eventually he took a second-floor apartment in the Ken Garden complex in Aberdeen

County, where neighbors described him as a quiet loner. A fan of industrial music and engrossed in the Internet, he often stayed in his apartment for long periods of time. He found work as a network programmer for a company that writes software for telecommunications giant AT&T. In his spare time Smith wrote a manual titled "Theory of Better File Virus Distribution."

MELISSA STARTS OFF WITH A BANG

The Melissa virus struck on March 26, 1999. It took only three minutes to transmit. By Monday, March 29, it had spread across the globe to computers in Belgium, Germany, China, and elsewhere. More than one million computers—including hundreds of networks—were affected by the virus. Were it not for well-publicized warnings that weekend, Melissa would have had an even greater impact.

Melissa first appeared as a message on a frequently visited sex newsgroup on the Internet. Computer users who visited that site downloaded a file containing passwords to other sex Web sites—as well as the Melissa virus. Robert Slade explained in *U.S. News & World Report* why such newsgroups provide an ideal starting-point for computer viruses. "Sending a virus to a sex-related newsgroup seems to be a reliable way to ensure that a large number of stupid people will read and execute your program, and start your new virus off with a bang."

MACRO MANIA

The Melissa virus took advantage of macros in Microsoft Word 97 and Word 2000. Macros are small programs that run specific tasks, such as running a search-and-replace function. Although macros normally cannot be embedded in e-mail, they can be attached to an e-mail file.

Recipients e-mail carrying the Melissa virus found a friendly looking message waiting in their in-boxes. The message was sent from a familiar e-mail address and the subject line indicated that the contents of the e-mail were important. The message read, "Here is the document you asked for...don't show anyone

A Brief History of Viruses

Macros are short programs that automate computer tasks. Hackers do not need to know extensive computer code to write a macro virus. In fact, some hackers even download virus code from the Internet.

Early computer viruses spread very slowly, taking months or even years to circulate around the world. They were spread through infected floppy discs, which were passed from one computer user to another. The popularity of e-mail helped facilitate the spread of viruses. Today, more than fifty million e-mail messages are sent every day. Because of this volume, viruses attached to e-mails can spread across the world in a matter of hours. The Melissa epidemic reached computers from Belgium to China in only seventy-two hours.

"Not everybody sees these people as bad guys or wants them punished," wrote Russell Mitchell in *U.S. News & World Report.* "Some programmers even argue that virus writers provide a public service, forcing the computer industry—and computer users—to wake up to the virus threat before a terrorist inflicts real mayhem."

else;-)." Attached to the e-mail was a Microsoft Word document named "list.doc."

Once the recipient opened the file, he or she became a victim of Melissa. As soon as the file was opened, the virus exploited Word macros that work with Microsoft Outlook, a program that organizes e-mail. Using the macros, the Melissa virus would attach itself to the first fifty e-mail addresses in the victim's Outlook address book. Some victims received multiple mailings of the Melissa virus. In fact, one computer user in Ann Arbor, Michigan, received 150 Melissa messages. "If your e-mail address started with A," she told *U.S. News & World Report,* "you were in trouble" (because names beginning with A are usually at the beginning of users' address books).

SYSTEM OVERLOAD

Unlike many viruses, Melissa did not damage victims' hard drives or data files; it simply overloaded systems by replicating itself again and again. With e-mail operations overloaded, victims were forced to shut down all computer operations. Tens of thousands of computer users, including large business and government agencies, were affected by the virus. Among Melissa's victims were the U.S. Marine Corps; Lockheed Martin Corporation, a leading defense contractor; the Veterans Administration; the headquarters of NATO (North Atlantic Treaty Organization); Microsoft; and the Intel Corporation.

For most, the virus was no more than an inconvenience. For others, however, the virus caused computer down-time that resulted in both direct and indirect damages. While prosecutors settled on a sum of $80,000 in damages, experts estimate that the virus cost businesses far more in terms of lost productivity of workers. According to the computer security firm ICSA Inc., lost productivity acquired $393 million in damages.

INVESTIGATORS CLOSE IN

The Melissa virus was tracked by an unusual assortment of computer sleuths. America Online and the New Jersey Attorney General's office joined forces with computer virus experts and the Federal Bureau of Investigation (FBI) to trace the virus to its creator. Richard M. Smith (no relation to David Smith), a computer security expert in Brookline, Massachusetts, identified a Microsoft source code that provided a "fingerprint" of the virus's creator.

Richard Smith posted the source code, called GUID (Globally Unique Identifier), on the Internet, where it drew the attention of a Swedish computer science graduate named Fredrik Bjork. Reviewing virus tool kit files on the Web site of another virus writer, Bjork discovered multiple references to David Smith.

Meanwhile, the New Jersey Attorney General's Computer Analysis and Technology Unit determined that Monmouth Internet Corporation, an Internet service provider (ISP) in Red Bank, New Jersey had relayed the initial Melissa message. After reviewing the company's files and customer transmissions, investigators discovered that the virus had been transmitted through a telephone line in David Smith's apartment. Smith had pirated, or broken into, an AOL user's account in order to disguise his own identity and used it to launch the virus from his apartment.

At dusk on April 1, 1999—less than a week after the launch of the virus—police and FBI agents descended on the Ken Garden apartment complex. Armed with a search warrant, they entered David Smith's empty apartment. They left with the suspect's computer and boxes filled with documents. A short while later, at 9:10 p.m., police arrested Smith at his brother's house in Eatontown. He put up no resistance.

TRIED AND CONVICTED

Although the state of New Jersey dropped charges of theft of computer services, Smith pled guilty to the state's charge of computer theft and the federal charge of "transmitting any program, code, document or other item with the purpose of damaging a computer program or data." If given the maximum sentences, he faced $480,000 in fines and forty years in jail.

"I did not expect or anticipate the amount of damage that's occurred," Smith told Superior Court Judge John A. Ricciardi (quoted in *The Record*). "When I posted the virus, I expected that any financial injury would be minor and incidental. In fact, I included features designed to prevent substantial damage. I had no idea there would be such a profound consequence to others."

The prosecution disagreed. "These crimes are not victimless crimes," State Attorney General John J. Farmer told *The Record*. "This paralyzed worldwide communications. I think he intended to do what he accomplished—a disruption of worldwide communication." The court agreed and Smith was convicted on December 10, 1999. He was sentenced to five years in prison and fined $5,000.

A Dubious Honor

David Smith was the first person in U.S. history to be prosecuted for designing a computer virus. But he was not the first to appear before a judge. In 1988 a federal judge had fined a virus writer in Maryland $10,000 for having caused six thousand computers to crash.

For More Information

Gold, Jeffrey. "Computer-Virus Maker Pleads Guilty." *The Fresno (California) Bee* (December 10, 1999).

Hawaleshka, Danylo. "Melissa's Message: A Nasty Computer Virus Could Have Been Worse." *Maclean's* (April 12, 1999).

Heyboer, Kelly. "Rutgers Baffled to Find 'Melissa' Hacker on Payroll." *The (Newark, NJ) Star-Ledger* (December 11, 1999).

Levy, Steven. "Biting Back at the Wily Melissa." *Newsweek* (April 12, 1999).

Locieniewski, David. "Man Is Charged in the Creation of E-Mail Virus." *New York Times* (April 3, 1999).

"Man Pleads Guilty to Loosing Melissa Virus." *Seattle Post-Intelligencer* (December 10, 1999).

"Melissa Worm Author Sentenced to 20 Months." *Sophos.* http://www.sophos.com/pressoffice/pressrel/uk/20020501smith.html (accessed on August 2, 2002).

Mitchell, Russell. "Why Melissa Is So Scary." *U.S. News & World Report* (April 12, 1999).

Sforza, Daniel. "N.J. Creator of Melissa Virus Pleads Guilty." *The (Bergen County, NJ) Record* (December 10, 1999).

Taylor, Chris. "How They Caught Him." *Time* (April 12, 1999).

The Sundance Kid

(Harry Longabaugh)

1867
c. November 6, 1908

AKA: Frank Boyd, Harry Place, "Enrique" Place

Bandit and Gunslinger

It is still unknown whether the two men killed by Bolivian policemen on November 6, 1908, were Butch Cassidy and the Sundance Kid.

Reproduced by permission of Archive Photos, Inc.

Harry Alonzo Longabaugh was best known as the Sundance Kid. He was a member of the Wild Bunch, a notorious band of robbers who roamed the Rocky Mountains in the 1890s robbing banks and trains. The Kid and his friend, **Butch Cassidy** (see entry in volume 3), eventually broke from the group and escaped detectives by moving to South America. Many believe they died in a final shootout with Bolivian soldiers in 1908.

THE LONGABAUGH KID

Longabaugh was born in Pennsylvania in the spring of 1867. The youngest of five children in a Baptist family, he left home when he was fifteen years old to live with relatives in Colorado. Later, he drifted around the U.S. and Canadian Rockies, working as a broncobuster and horse-driver. He was arrested in 1887 and served eighteen months in jail for horse theft. The jail was in Sundance, Wyoming, and it became the source of his nickname, the Sundance Kid.

Known as an expert shot, The Kid began to rob banks and trains with various other bandits. On June 27, 1897, he joined

Harvey Logan, Tom O'Day, and Walt Putney to rob a bank in Belle Fourche, South Dakota. The four robbers were captured and held in jail to wait for trial. On October 21, 1897, shortly before their trial date, The Kid and Logan escaped.

By 1900, The Kid had hooked up with Butch Cassidy and the Wild Bunch—a loose group of outlaws who roamed the Rocky Mountains robbing trains, banks, and payrolls. Between

1889 and 1901, the Wild Bunch reportedly collected more than $200,000—a sum worth more than $2.5 million today.

A PICTURE WORTH A THOUSAND WARRANTS

On December 1, 1900, the Wild Bunch celebrated their good luck by dressing in fine clothes to have a group picture taken in Fort Worth, Texas. This proved to be a serious mistake. Armed with the photograph, detectives from the noted Pinkerton agency and other law enforcers were better able to track and identify the members of the gang. With the help of witnesses, officials would be able to tie members of the Wild Bunch to their crimes.

One by one, the Wild Bunch began to fall captive to the lawmen who pursued them. On November 8, 1901, Ben Kilpatrick was arrested in St. Louis by detectives who recognized him from the Fort Worth photograph. The following month, Harvey Logan was arrested in Knoxville, Tennessee. Only three members of the Wild Bunch remained free: The Sundance Kid, Butch Cassidy, and O. C. Hanks.

SOUTH AMERICAN EXILE

Cassidy decided the time had come to move to South America. There, they would find mountainous terrain, open spaces, and weather similar to that of the American West. Further, the large numbers of foreigners in some South American countries would allow them to blend in with the population.

Cassidy, still the gang's decision maker, decided they would travel on a freight steamer because the threat of being detected would be too great on a passenger boat. The group was to set sail from New York to Buenos Aires, Argentina—a large port where they could slip into the country unnoticed. (Passports were not required for foreign travel at that time.)

How and when the outlaws traveled to South America is a matter of debate. According to one account, Cassidy, The Kid, and The Kid's wife Ethel, also known as Etta Place, set sail for Buenos Aires on the S.S. *Soldier Prince* on February 20, 1902. The Kid and Etta traveled as Mr. and Mrs. Harry D. Place, while Cassidy took the name James T. Ryan, posing as the brother of Mrs. Place. Another account has The Kid and Place arriving in

The Kid's Gal Pal

Sometime before leaving North America, The Kid met a woman known as Etta Place. Not much is known about the mysterious Ms. Place. According to some accounts, she was a married schoolteacher. Others identify her as a prostitute. Most claim she was uncommonly beautiful.

The Pinkerton detective agency identified her as the wife of The Kid—although no evidence suggests that the couple were married. Some say she was originally Cassidy's girlfriend but these reports, too, have never been proven.

Not even Place's name is a matter of record. The Pinkerton agency referred to her by various first names, including Etta, Ethel, and Eva. It is possible that the name "Place" was really an assumed name. The Kid's mother's maiden name was Place, too. Coincidence? Maybe.

As for the ultimate resting place of Etta Place, there is as much speculation about her final days as there is about that of Butch and Sundance. Some accounts describe her returning to the United States in 1907. Others have her moving to Paraguay, where she was said to have married a government official and raised a family. Yet another account claims she moved to Waco, Texas, where she died in a fire in 1962. No accounts, however, provide any definitive proof of what happened to her, leaving the mystery of Etta Place unsolved.

Argentine aboard the S.S. *Herminius* in 1901, to be joined by Cassidy the following year.

O. C. Hanks, who had remained in the United States, was killed in 1902 in a barroom fight. His death marked the end of the Wild Bunch's notorious reign among criminals in the American West. Not one member of the gang remained at large. Some were dead, others were in jail, and three lived in exile (forced or voluntary separation from one's native country) in South America.

ENRIQUE AND SANTIAGO'S EXCELLENT ADVENTURE

After landing in Buenos Aires, Argentina, Sundance, Cassidy, and Place took a train south to Patagonia (a mountainous region in southern Chile and Argentina), where they settled in a little-populated area called Chubut Territory (now a province of Argentina). Using the names Mr. and Mrs. "Enrique" Place and James "Santiago" Ryan, the trio moved to a ranch in the Cholila Valley. For a couple of years, they lived peacefully in a four-room log cabin on the ranch and raised horses, cows, and sheep.

Meanwhile, the Pinkerton detectives had received word that Cassidy and others had fled to Argentina. They sent detective Frank Dimaio, who had been working in Brazil, to track the outlaws in Argentina. Dimaio was able to determine where the bandits had settled, but the region's rainy season prevented him from traveling to Patagonia. He cabled the Pinkerton agency in New York to inform them that he would have to abandon the search. Before leaving, however, he arranged to have 150 wanted posters, showing photographs of The Kid, Cassidy, and Place, translated into Spanish and posted across the region.

Historians speculate that someone might have informed the outlaws that the Pinkertons were closing in on them. Others speculate that boredom or lack of funds prompted them to move. For whatever reason, the remnants of the Wild Bunch pulled up stakes in Cholila early in 1905. Soon thereafter, English-speaking bandits began to rob Argentinean banks of their funds.

ENGLISH-SPEAKING BANDITS

On February 14, 1905, in the broad daylight of 3 p.m., two English-speaking robbers held up the Banco de Londres y Tarapaca in Rio Gallegos, about 700 miles (1,126 kilometers) south of Cholila, in the Santa Cruz Territory. Collecting paper currency, coins, and British sterling, the two men escaped on horseback. Heading north, they evaded mounted police who searched in vain across difficult terrain. Although the robbers were never positively identified, The Kid and Cassidy were considered the primary suspects.

In late 1905, the Banco de la Nación in Villa Mercedes (400 miles, or 644 kilometers, west of Buenos Aires) was robbed of 12,000 pesos—worth more than $100,000 today. Witnesses claimed that the four robbers, suspected to be Cassidy, The Kid, Place, and an unknown man, had been seen in town earlier—speaking English and drinking American whiskey. Five days after the robbery, on December 24, two newspapers in Buenos Aires published stories about the criminal history of three members of the Wild Bunch: Cassidy, The Kid, and Harry "Kid Curry" Logan. The Pinkerton agency provided photographs of the Wild Bunch, along with their associate Etta Place, for the articles.

The search for the Wild Bunch, and their associate Etta Place, intensified. Before long, Cassidy, The Kid, and Place crossed the Andes Mountains to seek haven in Chile. Although no documents provide any clue to what they did when they first arrived there, the bandits eventually made their way to the northern seaport of Antofagasta, where the town's many foreign residents made it easy to avoid detection. At some point during this time, Place left the two outlaws, either to return to the United States or to strike out on her own in South America.

TIN MINES AND HIGHWAY ROBBERS

In 1907 Cassidy and The Kid made their way from Chile to Bolivia, where they introduced themselves as James "Santiago" Maxwell and Frank Boyd or H. A. "Enrique" Brown. The two eventually worked for the Concordia Tin Mine, 16,000 feet (25,745 meters) high in the Bolivian Andes. As far as records indicate, the two outlaws—whose responsibilities included guarding the mine's payroll—were upstanding employees. Their boss, Percy Seibert was an engineer from Maryland who had worked at numerous mining camps in Bolivia. He later reported that the two had been model employees, although they considered the payrolls of other companies to be fair game. In 1908 the pair quit their jobs at the tin mine—possibly, as legend has it, because The Kid revealed too much about his criminal past while drunk.

On November 4, 1908, the manager of a mining company called Armayo, Francke, and Company was held up by two masked men. The manager, Carlos Pero, was intercepted as he took the company's payroll from the Tupiza office to the company headquarters in Quechisla. Accompanying him were his young son, Mariano, and a servant. According to company records, the two masked robbers were tall, well-armed men who carried guns, rifles, and plenty of ammunition. They were polite when they asked Pero to hand over the company payroll, totaling 15,000 Bolivian pesos (more than $90,000 today).

SHOWDOWN AT SAN VICENTE

After the robbers left, Pero sped to a mining camp, where he sent a telegram notifying his employers of the theft. Before the day ended, law enforcement officials throughout the southern portion of Bolivia had been notified of the robbery. Initially,

Pero claimed the heist had been committed by a thin "gringo" (American, or Yankee) and a heavy Chilean by the name of Madariaga. He later changed his story to identify both robbers as gringos—both of whom had approached him for work prior to the robbery.

On November 6, 1908, three days after the hold-up, a posse of Bolivian soldiers found the fugitives in San Vicente, not far from Bolivia's borders with neighboring Chile and Argentina. The soldiers, led by Captain Justo P. Concha, traded fire with the two outlaws. When the skirmish ended, two lawmen and both outlaws had been killed. Concha and the remaining policeman recovered the stolen payroll.

Two days later, Bolivian newspapers reported that two foreigners had robbed the Armayo, Francke, and Company payroll. Few agreed on the identity of the outlaws, who were alternately described as North Americans, Danes, and Chileans. Unable to positively identify the two dead men, officials had them buried together in the same grave.

A GRAVE MATTER

Popular legend identified Cassidy and The Kid as the outlaws who died in the November 6, 1908, shootout with Bolivian soldiers. But no records provide concrete proof that the two Wild Bunch bandits were those who exchanged gunfire with soldiers that day. Nor do records offer any proof that they were the two dead fugitives who were buried in the San Vicente cemetery.

In fact, modern science ruled out the possibility that Cassidy and The Kid were laid to rest in San Vicente. In 1991 the PBS television program *Nova* arranged to have the San Vicente grave dug up. After the remains were removed from the grave, DNA tests were performed. Scientists determined that the skeletal remains belonged to neither Cassidy nor The Kid.

What actually became of Butch Cassidy and The Sundance Kid is a matter of speculation. William A. Pinkerton, of the Pinkerton detective agency, never believed that the pair had died in San Vicente, and his agency continued for years to hunt for them in South America. Stories of the bandits' deaths continued to circulate: Cassidy was killed in a barroom fight somewhere in the tropics; he was stabbed to death in the streets of Paris; he was shot in a brothel in New Mexico. The Kid was said to have been killed with Cassidy; but it was also reported that he had been gunned down by police in Argentina, Bolivia, and Chile. Another story had him killed by a friend in Venezuela. Still other stories have the famous outlaws returning to the United States to live peacefully to ripe old age. There may never be a way to be certain what happened to two of the most infamous outlaws ever.

For More Information

Browne, Malcolm W. "Scientists Hunt Down 2 Outlaws and Find 2 Skeletons." *New York Times* (January 17, 1992): p. A-12.

Buck, Daniel, and Anne Meadows. "The Last Days of Butch and Sundance." *Wild West* (February 1997): p. 36.

Buck, Daniel, and Anne Meadows. "The Many Deaths of Butch and Sundance." *Wild West* (February 1997): p. 40.

Grose, Thomas K., et al. "The Butler Didn't Do It." *U.S. News & World Report* (July 24, 2000): p. 80.

Hollon, W. Eugene. *The New Encyclopedia of the American West.* New Haven, CT: Yale University Press, 1988, pp. 888–889.

Meadows, Anne, and Daniel Buck. "Running Down a Legend." *Americas,* English edition (November–December 1990): p. 21.

Swallow, Alan. *The Wild Bunch.* Denver, CO: Sage Books, 1966, pp. 30, 49–50, 58–59, 61, 63, 70–73, 74, 80, 83, 89, 93, 100.

William Sutton Jr.

June 30, 1901
November 2, 1980

AKA: The Actor

Robber

"Why did I rob banks? Because I enjoyed it. I loved it. I was more alive when I was inside a bank, robbing it, than at any other time in my life."

—Willie Sutton,
quoted in *ABA
Banking Journal*

Willie "The Actor" Sutton spent two years on the Federal Bureau of Investigation's (FBI's) Ten Most Wanted List. He was known to disguise himself as a police officer to gain entry to the banks he robbed. After spending thirty-three years in prison, his notoriety helped him get a new job—as spokesperson for a bank.

A WORKING-CLASS UPBRINGING

Born on June 30, 1901, William "Willie" Francis Sutton, Jr. was raised in the Irishtown section of Brooklyn, New York. His mother, Mary Ellen Bowles Sutton, a native of Ireland, was deeply religious and his father, William Francis Sutton Sr., was a blacksmith. Sutton grew up in a working-class extended family that included his maternal grandfather and two uncles. His mother's sister-in-law lived with the family as well, and exercised considerable influence over her young nephew. A cultured and attractive woman, Aunt Alice taught Sutton how to carry himself, dress well, and practice good manners.

The Doc Was My Mentor

Like many bank robbers, Sutton learned the tricks of his trade from an experienced teacher, or mentor—a bank robber called Doc Tate. Sutton told *Life* magazine how he admired this man: "Doc was probably the greatest expert on locks in the country. A real practitioner, he always wore gloves, even in the warmest weather, to protect his sensitive fingertips. I began to learn the difference between amateurs like myself and professionals like Doc Tate. He had been caught many times. But each time he asked himself, 'What did I do wrong? What precaution did I fail to take?' And he never made the same mistake twice.

"I became Doc's eager student. After a while he let me go along on jobs, in Boston, Scranton and Wilkes-Barre [Pennsylvania]. From him I learned my most valuable lessons: Use nitro and the blowtorch only when the 'legitimate' ways—the punch, jimmy, and other tools—fail. Do an out-of-town job, then get as far away as possible as fast as possible. Use ordinary tools, the kind that can be bought in any hardware store, and leave them behind—except the jimmy, which will get you out of many a tight, locked place. Choose your fence with the greatest of care. And plan, plan, plan. The Doc was my mentor. But I'm convinced that becoming a criminal was my fault, not his. The Doc only helped me become a successful criminal—for a while."

Attending both public and private schools, Sutton proved to be a bright student with good grades and a good memory. He finished grammar school just after the United States became involved in World War I (1914–18). With so many men overseas with the military, jobs at home were plentiful. Sutton chose employment over continuing his education through high school. He took a job as an office boy and later worked in a weapons factory. During this period he tried to enlist in the army, but the war ended before the draft board called him to service.

FROM PETTY THEFT TO GRAND LARCENY

A spirited boy, Sutton found trouble at an early age. He committed his first theft as a child, when he took a quarter from a drawer in his grandfather's dresser so that he could buy a pigeon. After the bird flew away, he confessed to the old man, who gave him another quarter.

At age ten, Sutton and a friend broke into a small department store by climbing through a skylight. Climbing down a rope ladder into the store, they burgled the store and later entertained their friends with the money they had taken. Two years later, he was in trouble for stealing lunch money from one of his teachers. A short while later, he lost his job as a mail clerk at an insurance company because he was caught stealing stamps.

Sutton committed his first major crime when he was seventeen years old. When Sutton and his fifteen-year-old girlfriend, Carrie Wagner, expressed their desire to marry, her father objected. The couple then planned to elope (run away to get married) and Sutton planned to finance their life together with money stolen from Wagner's father's business. With a vault key provided by his girlfriend, Sutton took $16,000 from his prospective father-in-law. The couple boarded a train for Albany, New York, and then bought a car. They traveled around the East Coast, finally landing in Poughkeepsie, New York, where they were recognized and arrested. Sutton was sentenced to one year in a reformatory but was granted a suspension. In exchange, he agreed to find a job and to stop seeing Wagner. He did as promised, but also carried out some bank robberies on the side.

THE VIRTUE OF DISGUISE

In July 1921 Sutton, accused of murdering a man he had quarreled with, fled to Manhattan and changed his name. Once settled in New York City, he began studying safe-cracking. Working as an appliance repairman, he turned his attention to the mechanics of alarm systems. He experimented with blow torches as a way to open steel safes. He also began to explore the art of makeup and disguise—a practice that would become the signature of his later career.

In 1923 Sutton was arrested. Charged with robbery and murder, he spent nine months in jail awaiting trial. To the surprise of many, he was found not guilty. (Sutton later claimed in his autobiography that he did not commit the murder.) But it was not long before Sutton was behind bars again. In 1926 he and partner Eddie Wilson attempted to rob the Ozone National

Bank in Queens, New York. Having abandoned the job because it was taking too long, the two were involved in a car accident as they fled the scene. Sutton and Wilson were arrested and convicted of burglary and attempted grand larceny (theft).

Sutton was sentenced to five to ten years at Sing Sing prison in Ossining, New York. Having survived three months in the brutal atmosphere of Sing Sing, he was transferred to Dannemora Prison in northeastern New York. In August 1929, just days after a prison riot, he was paroled (released early and under certain conditions).

Sutton made a practice of analyzing his failures. "I was thinking about my failure to relieve the Ozone Park Bank of the contents of its vault," he later wrote in his autobiography. "I was

The two guns on the desk, above, were found in the possession of bank robber Willie "The Actor" Sutton, second from left, when he was arrested while changing his car battery. *Reproduced by permission of AP/Wide World Photos.*

walking along Broadway when I saw an armored truck stop in front of a business establishment after closing hours. Two of the uniformed guards approached the door, rang the bell, and were admitted. In a few moments they marched from the store, climbed into their truck and drove off.... I doubted very much if the clerk who admitted them to the store looked at their faces. He saw the uniforms and waved them in. The right uniform was an open sesame...that would unlock any door. That afternoon 'Willie the Actor' was born."

CLOTHES MAKE THE MAN

On October 21, 1929, just months after his release from prison, Sutton married Louise Leudemann. The couple had one child, a daughter named Jeanne, who rarely saw her father because of his frequent imprisonment.

Using phony stationary from a non-existent school of art and drama, Sutton began to gather makeup and costumes. Donning the appropriate uniform or disguise, he posed as a workman, messenger, fireman, or policeman in order to gain entry to the jewelry stores and banks he intended to rob. Well-versed in the tricks of the theater trade, he became known as the Actor.

Sutton left his wife and young daughter in New York, where they lived in a home on Long Island, and he moved to Philadelphia, Pennsylvania. With his family safe at a distance, he continued his career as a disguised bank robber.

By 1933 Sutton was again locked up, having been sentenced to time in Pennsylvania's Eastern State Prison. Four failed escapes and a hunger strike landed him in Holmesburg, a maximum security prison in Philadelphia. On February 3, 1947, Sutton and four other inmates proved that the "escape-proof" Holmesburg Prison did not live up to its reputation. Disguised as guards, the five inmates climbed over the prison wall and escaped under cover of a driving snowstorm.

WHERE THE MONEY WAS

In Staten Island, New York, Sutton took a job at a home for the elderly. But he continued to rob banks on the side. On March 9, 1950, he stole $60,000 from the Manufacturer's Trust Bank, earning himself a spot on the FBI's Ten Most Wanted list. For two years, Sutton remained at large. But on February 10, 1952, while he was riding a train to Brooklyn, he was recognized by Arnold Schuster, a twenty-four-year-old worker in a tailor shop. Alerted to Sutton's whereabouts by Schuster, the police arrested the bank robber as he changed the battery in his car.

On March 9, 1952, shortly after appearing on television to discuss the apprehension of Sutton, Arnold Schuster was found shot to death. Sutton was cleared of any involvement in the murder. Many believe the death was a killing-for-hire contracted by mob boss Albert Anastasia, who was angered by Schuster's actions and considered him a "squealer"—someone who helps out police by giving them information about criminals. Convicted of the 1950 bank robbery, Sutton, now fifty-one years old, was sentenced to a minimum of thirty years in prison.

Sutton spent much of his prison time studying law. The former bank robber, who as a child had dreamed of becoming a criminal lawyer, helped fellow inmates with legal research and appeal-writing. With the help of writer Quentin Reynolds, Sutton began to compose his autobiography, *I, Willie Sutton,* which he dedicated to his daughter.

On December 24, 1969, Sutton was released from prison on parole. Believed to have been involved in the robberies of one hundred banks, work was hard to come by. He was forced to apply for welfare to get by. He moved to Spring Hill, Florida, to live with his sister. There he set to work on his second autobiography, *Where the Money Was, The Memoirs of a Bank Robber,* which was written with Edward Linn. An acknowledged expert in the field of breaking and entering, Sutton acted as a security consultant for banks and lectured on

Willie Sutton, Actor

Sutton knew that the right uniform would unlock any door—providing an "open sesame" to whatever bank or jewelry store he set in his sights. But he also realized there was much more to the art of disguise than simply wearing the right clothes. He sometimes walked with a limp or talked with a lisp to create a false identity. He also wore elevated shoes to appear taller, and applied fake scars, warts, and facial hair. He dyed his hair different colors and used makeup to change the tone of his complexion. Sutton even changed the contour of his nose by placing hollowed-out corks in his nostrils.

prison reform. Ironically he even made a television commercial for a bank, promoting their credit card with the line, "Now when I say I'm Willie Sutton, people believe me." Sutton died on November 2, 1980, and was buried in an unmarked grave in Brooklyn, New York.

For More Information

Axthelm, Pete. "The Game Willie Played." *Newsweek* (December 1, 1980).

Cocheo, Steve. "The Bank Robber, the Quote, and the Final Irony." *ABA Banking Journal* 89 (March 1997): pp. 71–72.

Dictionary of American Biography. Supplement 10: 1976–1980. New York: Charles Scribner's Sons, 1995.

"One on One; Voices from Life." *Life* (fall 1986) vol. 9: p. 117.

Sifakis, Carl. *The Encyclopedia of American Crime.* 2d ed. New York: Facts on File, 2001, pp. 859–860.

Charles Whitman

1941
August 1, 1966

Mass Murderer

On August 1, 1966, Charles Whitman, a married University of Texas architectural engineering student, carried weapons and supplies into the U of T tower and opened fire on students below. He killed fifteen people and wounded thirty-one others in the span of an hour and a half.

BEHIND THE PICKET FENCE

To most observers, Whitman appeared to be the all-American boy-next-door type. The oldest of three sons of a plumbing contractor, he grew up in Lake Worth, Florida. He attended Catholic school and served as an altar boy. A talented athlete, he played sports, had a paper route, and became an Eagle Scout at age twelve.

But Whitman's childhood had been far from ideal. His father had a short temper and subjected his sons to harsh discipline and often beat his wife. Throughout his life, Whitman nurtured an intense hatred for the man who, in his opinion, had ruined his mother's life.

"The Whitman attack marked a new and different terror--that anyone anywhere could be killed at random."

--Jim Yardley, reporting for the *New York Times*

153

Embracing the Positive

The observation deck of the tower at the University of Texas, from where Whitman shot at innocent passersby, was closed in 1975, following several suicides from that site. But on September 16, 1999, on the university's 116th birthday, the tower was reopened with security checkpoints and stainless steel lattice to prevent people from jumping. Dr. Kenneth Foote, a geography professor at the university since 1982 told reporters, "I think it's time for this university to move on and accept the history that goes with this building and fully embrace the positives." On August 1, 1999—thirty-three years after the shooting— university officials dedicated a garden at the base of the tower in memory of the victims of Whitman's rampage.

As a student at the University of Texas, Whitman maintained close to an A average. In the summer of 1966, as a married junior majoring in architectural engineering, he carried an especially difficult course load. He was under stress, and it showed. He suffered from intense headaches and his short temper gave way to sudden bursts of violence. Like his father, he had beaten his wife. Whitman's behavior was dismissed as the product of stress. But no one suspected how close he was to the breaking point.

A TROUBLED YOUNG MAN OOZING HOSTILITY

Whitman was aware that something was wrong. On March 29, 1966, he went to see the school's staff psychologist to discuss his violent temper. He admitted to beating his wife and told the doctor that he had trouble controlling his temper. He claimed that he was afraid that he might become uncontrollably violent and he mentioned thoughts of shooting people from the university tower.

The doctor was not surprised by Whitman's fantasy. He later claimed that many students who visited the clinic focused on the tower as the site of some "desperate action." He also noted that Whitman "seemed to be oozing hostility," and asked him to return for another visit. But Whitman never went back to the clinic.

The troubled young man had other plans. On July 31, he began to type a note outlining his plan of action. He explained that he had been battling fears and violent feelings—and that these feelings had driven him to a final act of violence. He also indicated that he planned to kill his wife in order to spare her from the shame of what he was about to do.

Whitman was interrupted by friends who stopped by his home. When Mr. and Mrs. Fuess spoke to him, he gave no indication of what he planned to do. In fact, Mr. Fuess noted that his friend had seemed "particularly relieved about something…as if he had solved a problem."

A STRANGE WAY TO SHOW HIS LOVE

Whitman next picked up his wife from her job at the telephone company and dropped her at home. He then drove to his mother's apartment. There he stabbed his mother with a butcher knife and shot her in the back of the head. Before leaving, he wrote a short note, in which he explained that he had put an end to his mother's suffering. In closing, he wrote that he loved his mother "with all my heart."

Hundreds of students ran for cover when sniper Charles Whitman opened fire from the University of Texas tower, killing fifteen people and wounding thirty-one others. *Reproduced by permission of Corbis Corporation.*

A Dangerous Tumor?

In the encyclopedia *Violence in America* (edited by Ronald Gottesman), the possible connection between Whitman's brain tumor and his shooting spree is explored in scientific terms:

Most evidence indicating that the limbic structures [brain structures involved with memory and emotion] contribute to aggression is drawn from research on non-human mammals. In the 1930s the work of Kluver and Bucy revealed that damage to the amygdala [region of the brain] produced dramatic changes in emotional and social behaviors in monkeys. Specifically, monkeys that were previously highly aggressive became very passive following damage to the amygdala. Further, electrical stimulation of the particular regions of the amygdala and the hypothalamus has been shown to have an excitatory influence on aggressive behavior in cats. There appears to be little doubt that these structures are intimately involved in the control of both affective (defensive) and predatory aggression.

On the basis of studies of these animal models, scientists have speculated that abnormalities in the amygdala and hypothalamus may be responsible for serious violent behavior in humans. For example, Charles Whitman was later found to have been suffering from an amygdaloid tumor [a growth in the amygdala region]. However, it is not clear what, if any, effect the tumor had on his behavior.

After returning home, Whitman found his wife in bed, sleeping. After stabbing her three times, he returned to his letter. He wrote about his intense hatred of his father, and expressed regret that his mother had wasted her life with him. He claimed that life was not worth living and that he was ready to die. But he had one final request. "I am prepared to die," he wrote. "After my death, I wish an autopsy on me to be performed to see if there is any mental disorder."

A SHOOTING GALLERY

Whitman had planned his final attack carefully. He loaded a footlocker with rifles, pistols, a revolver, a shotgun, and almost seven hundred rounds of ammunition. He also packed a duffel bag full of supplies. He included everything he would need throughout the upcoming day, including sandwiches, Spam, bottled water, toilet paper, binoculars, and a transistor radio. He also packed some deodorant, peanuts, and fruit cocktail.

Sometime after 11 a.m. on August 1, loaded with arms and supplies, Whitman headed for the observation deck of the university tower. On the twenty-seventh floor, he encountered Edna Townsley, a receptionist at the tower's information desk. After killing her with a blow from the butt of his rifle, he barricaded the stairway, and made his way up to the observation deck. As he started to lay out his gear, a group of sightseers stepped onto the deck. Whitman opened fire on the unsuspecting visitors, killing or injuring most of them. Those who were still standing retreated to the twenty-seventh floor.

After blocking the door to the observation deck, Whitman began shooting at people below. The time was about 11:45 a.m.—shortly after the 11:30 a.m. change of classes brought many more people to the area. Firing from various angles in the tower, Whitman randomly injured and killed his victims from his perch above campus.

His aim was astonishing. As a child, he had learned from his father how to handle and shoot guns, and time in the Marine Corps had turned him into an expert marksman. Shooting from an average distance of 300 feet (91 meters), he struck his target at least once out of every three shots. During the next hour and thirty-six minutes, he killed fifteen people and injured thirty-one others. Most were struck during the first twenty minutes of the rampage.

AMBUSHED AND AUTOPSIED

Whitman's victims included students, law officers, children, and other civilians. One of the first to be hit was an eighteen-year-old pregnant student. She survived, but her baby was killed—as was her husband, who rushed to her side to help her. Also killed were a Peace Corps trainee, a paperboy, and an Austin policeman named Billy Speed, among others.

The police, who were notified of the ambush within four minutes of the first shot, found it difficult to target the gunman. Stationed behind the tower walls, Whitman shot through drainage slits, making it virtually impossible for police to hit him from below. Texas Rangers, Secret Service agents, and

Live, on Channel 2

The University of Texas shooting marked a significant turning point in news reporting. As the event unfolded, a television reporter name Neal Spelce narrated raw footage of the shooting spree—foreshadowing the sort of media coverage that is common today.

highway patrolmen joined the more than one hundred city police who rallied to stop the rampage.

Convinced that they needed another plan of attack, police organized an air strike. They sent expert marksmen in a small chartered plane to target the shooter from above. Looking down at the tower, the marksmen shot at Whitman, but his return fire drove them away.

Eventually, three policemen, along with a former Air Force gunner named Allen Crum, were able to enter the tower building. After climbing the stairway to the observation deck, they forced their way through the barricaded door. Entering on the south side of the deck, they surrounded Whitman from the east and west. A brief exchange of gunfire left the gunman dead and Austin patrolman Ramiro Martinez wounded. The time was 1:24 p.m.—just ninety-six minutes after Whitman's first shot had wrung out.

An autopsy revealed that Whitman had a tumor in the hypothalamus region of the brain (an area of the brain that regulates body temperature and some metabolic processes). Although doctors questioned whether the tumor had caused the young man's violent spree, some suspect that it was responsible for Whitman's erratic behavior.

For More Information

Gaute, J. H. H., and Robin Odell. *The New Murderers' Who's Who*. London: Harrap Books Ltd., 1979, 1989, p. 318.

Gottesman, Ronald, ed. *Violence in America: An Encyclopedia*. New York: Charles Scribner's Sons, 1999, vol. 3: pp. 454, 446–447.

Lavergne, Gary M. *A Sniper in the Tower: The Charles Whitman Murders*. Denton, TX: University of North Texas Press, 1997.

Layman, Richard, ed. *American Decades: 1960–1969*. Detroit, MI: Gale Research, 1995, pp. 286–288.

Sifakis, Carl. *The Encyclopedia of American Crime*. 2d ed. New York: Facts on File, 2001, vol. 2: pp. 943–945.

Yardley, Jim. "Off Limits Since '74, Deck Reopens." *New York Times* (September 16, 1999): National Desk.

Index

Italic type indicates volume number;
boldface *indicates main entries in Volume 5 and their page numbers;*
(ill.) indicates illustration.

Cannary, Martha Jane. *See* Calamity Jane

Capital punishment. *See* Death penalty

"Capo di Tutti Capi" *1:* 25

Capone, Al *1:* 13–20, 13 (ill.), 18 (ill.), 41, 54, 87; *3:* 420, 425, 446, 460, 466, 468; *4:* 6, 114–115

Capone, Louis *1:* 94

Capone, Ralph *3:* 423

Capuzzi, Nick *1:* 21

Cardinelli, Sam *1:* 8

Carl, Peter *2:* 187

Carnegie, Andrew *2:* 263

Carnegie Endowment for International Peace *4:* 71

The Carnegie Scam *2:* 263

Carnera, Primo *3:* 440, 440 (ill.)

Carranza, Venustiano *3:* 412

Carroll, Tommy *1:* 140; *4:* 6, 8

Carter, Bill *3:* 337

Carter, Jimmy *1:* 164; *4:* 65

Caruso, Enrico *1:* 9, 11 (ill.)

Caruso, Frank *1:* 5

Carver, William *3:* 368 (ill.)

Casper Weekly Mail 2: 255

Cassidy, Butch *3:* 367–375, 367 (ill.), 368 (ill.); *5:* 138, 139–145

Cassidy, George. *See* Cassidy, Butch

Cassidy, Mike *3:* 367

Cassidy, William *1:* 82

Castellano, Paul *1:* 21, 26, 37, 38

Castellano, Peter *1:* 21

Castiglia, Francesco. *See* Costello, Frank

Castro assassination plot *5:* 98

Castro, Fidel *1:* 32

Catalupo, Joseph *1:* 25

Catch Me If You Can 5: 1, 9

The Catcher in the Rye 4: 40–47

Cattle barons *2:* 254, 256; *3:* 348

Cattle Kate *2:* 253–260, 253 (ill.)

Caulfield, Holden *4:* 41, 42

Caverly, John *5:* 78–79

CBN (Christian Broadcasting Network) *4:* 14–16. *See also* Bakker, Jim

Cecil B. Demented 4: 66

Cellano, Margie. *See* Dean, Margie

Centennial Park bombing *5:* 118–119, 120 (ill.)

Central Intelligence Agency (CIA) *1:* 32; *2:* 218–219, 225; *4:* 48; *5:* 98

Cermak, Anton J. *4:* 117

Cerone, Jackie *1:* 5

Chadwick, Cassie *2:* 261–265, 261 (ill.), 262 (ill.)

Chadwick, Constance Cassandra. *See* Chadwick, Cassie

Chadwick, Leroy *2:* 263

Chambers, Edwin *5:* 56

Chambers, Sandra. *See* Kimes, Sante

Chambers, Whittaker *4:* 69, 71–73, 72 (ill.)

Chaos Computer Club *2:* 183, 185, 187

Chapman, Mark David *4:* 40–48, 40 (ill.)

Chase, John Paul *4:* 6, 8

Chemotherapy *5:* 42–43

Cherokee Nation *3:* 399

Chesimard, JoAnne *2:* 305–310, 305 (ill.), 309, 310

Chesimard, Louis *2:* 307

Chicago Crime Commission *1:* 33

Chicago organized crime *4:* 7–9, 115–116. *See also* Baby Face Nelson; Nitti, Frank

The Chicago Outfit *1:* 3, 5, 28–30

Christian Broadcasting Network (CBN) *4:* 14–16. *See also* Bakker, Jim

Christian Identity movement *5:* 121

Christy, Jim *2:* 187

Chubut Territory, Argentina *5:* 141–142

Church of the Brethren *5:* 80–81

Chuvakin, Sergei *2:* 217

CIA (Central Intelligence Agency) *1:* 32; *2:* 218–219, 225; *4:* 48; *5:* 98

Cicotte, Eddie *1:* 97

CIO (Congress of International Organizers) *4:* 78

Circolo Accera Club *1:* 84

Citizen Kane 1: 162

Citizens for Decent Literature *5:* 46

Civil disobedience *5:* 62, 63–65

Civil rights movement *5:* 36–37

Civil War, American. *See* American Civil War

Claire at Sixteen 2: 264

Clancy, Thomas *1:* 50 (ill.)

Clanton, Billy *4:* 52–54

Clanton, Ike *4:* 52, 53

Clanton-McLowry Gang *3:* 376, 382. *See also* O.K. Corral

Clarion-Ledger 5: 38

Clark, Arizona Donnie. *See* Barker, Ma

Clark, Russell Lee *1:* 136

Cleaners and Dyers War *1:* 55

Cleary, Robert *5:* 135

Climbing *4:* 127–132

Clinton, Bill *4:* 65, 120, 124–125, 125 (ill.); *5:* 106

Clinton, Hillary *4:* 125 (ill.)

Coakley, Daniel H. *5:* 95

Coast Diamond Distributors *2:* 206

Coburn, James *3:* 348

Code names *2:* 239. *See also* Spies

Cody, "Buffalo Bill" *3:* 365

Coe, Phil *4:* 160–161

Coffeyville bank robberies *5:* 31, 32

Cohen, Hymie *1:* 82

Cohen, Reuben *1:* 55

Cohen, Samuel *1:* 57

Colby, William *1:* 33

Coletta, Cuono *1:* 85

Coliseum Saloon and Variety Theatre *3:* 409

Coll, Peter *3:* 453

Federal witness protection program *5:* 42

Feklisov, Aleksander *2:* 236

The Female Offender 2: 288

Ferguson, Miriam "Ma" *1:* 123

Ferrero, William *2:* 288

Fetters (iron chains) *1:* 171

Findlay, Tom *4:* 138–139

First National Bank robbery *5:* 31

Firsts

    daylight bank robbery *3:* 388

    execution for espionage *2:* 242

    gangland funeral *3:* 468

    getaway drivers *1:* 130

    "Hands Up" used *1:* 173

    legalized gambling *1:* 62

    military use of mechanized vehicles *3:* 414

    prosecution of computer virus designer *5:* 137

    train robbery in Canada *1:* 176

    train robbery in Georgia *1:* 176

    train robbery in U.S. *3:* 344

    use of California's gas chamber *3:* 435

    woman executed *1:* 177

    woman tried for major crime *3:* 399

Fitzgerald, F. Scott *1:* 97

Fitzgerald, John *5:* 96

Fitzsimmons, Frank *4:* 82

Five Points Gang *1:* 13–15

"The Fixer." *See* Rothstein, Arnold

Flamingo Hotel *1:* 62

Flegenheimer, Arthur. *See* Schultz, Dutch

Fleischer, Harry *1:* 53, 54 (ill.)

Fleischer, Louis *1:* 53

Flemmi, Stephen "The Rifleman" *5:* 22–24, 23 (ill.)

Flesch, Oscar *1:* 97

Fletcher, Eddie *1:* 55 (ill.), 57

Florida Land Scam *2:* 295

Floyd, Charles Arthur. *See* Pretty Boy Floyd

Floyd, Pretty Boy. *See* Pretty Boy Floyd

Flynn, Billy *5:* 124, 126–129

Fogo, Fred *4:* 44

Foote, Kenneth *5:* 154

Ford, Bob *3:* 392 (ill.), 393

Ford, Charles *3:* 392

Ford, Henry *1:* 122

Ford, Robert *3:* 392

Foreign Miners' Tax *5:* 89

Forgery *5:* 8

Forrest, Nathan Bedford *3:* 333

Fort Sumner *3:* 350

Fortier, Michael *2:* 322

"Forty-niners" *3:* 338. *See also* California gold rush

42 Gang *1:* 3, 5, 28, 30

Foss, Nick *4:* 60

Foster, Marcus *1:* 158; *4:* 145

Fox, Richard *3:* 401

Francis, James *1:* 166

Franks, Bobby *5:* 76–77

Frasier 1: 161

Free climbing *4:* 128–132

Freedom Club *4:* 89, 90

Freeh, Louis J. *2:* 316

Friends of the Soviet Union *2:* 232

Frog Hollow Gang *3:* 452

Fuchs, Klaus *2:* 237

Fugitives

    Bulger, James *5:* **21–27,** 21 (ill.)

    Rudolph, Eric Robert *5:* **117–123,** 117 (ill.)

Fulton-Rockaway Boys *1:* 35

Fusco, Tony *1:* 80

G

Galente, Carmine *1:* 26

Galione, Ralphie *1:* 37

Galligher, Carl *5:* 112

Gallows *3:* 494. *See also* Death penalty

Gambino, Carlo *1:* 21–27, 21 (ill.), 22 (ill.), 33, 37

Gambino crime family *5:* 41

Gambino family chart *1:* 22 (ill.)

Gamblers. *See* Racketeers and gamblers

Gandil, Chick *1:* 97

Garcia, Andy *1:* 33

Garcia, Manuel *5:* 90

Gardner, Erle Stanley *5:* 80

Garlic-tipped bullets *3:* 425

Garrett, John *3:* 354

Garrett, Pat *3:* 350, 351 (ill.), 352–353

Geaquenta, Mack *1:* 85

Gelertner, David *4:* 89, 90

Genna, Angelo *3:* 424, 426, 445, 467

Genna, Antonio *3:* 424

The Genna Brothers *1:* 87; *3:* 420, 424–429, 445

Genna, Jim *3:* 424, 429

Genna, Mike *3:* 424, 427

Genna, Pete *3:* 424, 429

Genna, Sam *3:* 424, 429

Genna, Tony *3:* 425, 428

Genovese, Vito *1:* 23–24, 73; *2:* 232; *3:* 455

"Gentleman Johnnie." *See* Dillinger, John

George I *3:* 481

Giacalone, Tony *4:* 82

Giancana, Antonino *1:* 28

Giancana, Carlo *1:* 4

Giancana, Gilormo. *See* Giancana, Sam

Giancana, Sam *1:* 3–5, 28–34, 28 (ill.), 31 (ill.)

Gibbet cage *3:* 489

Gibbs, Charles *3:* 492–495, 492 (ill.)

Gigante, Vincent *1:* 73

Gillis, Helen Wawzynak *4:* 8, 10

Gillis, Lester J. *See* Baby Face Nelson

Ginter, Leonard *2:* 312–313

Ginter, Norma *2:* 312–313

M